Inspiring
ELEMENTARY
LEARNERS

To the children of today who will become the leaders of the future. We know that with the love and support of caring adults, you can become the change you wish to see in the world.

To our families who believe and support our vision of leaving the world a better place for the children. As Gandhi said, "If we are to have real peace, we must begin with the children."

To the visionaries, teachers, and leaders who are lighting the way and giving us courage and inspiration to build a new future.

Inspiring
ELEMENTARY
LEARNERS

Nurturing the Whole Child in a Differentiated Classroom

KATHLEEN KRYZA ~ ALICIA DUNCAN ~ S. JOY STEPHENS

CORWIN PRESS

A SAGE Company

For information:

Corwin Press
A SAGE Company
2455 Teller Road
Thousand Oaks, California 91320
www.corwinpress.com

SAGE India Pvt. Ltd.
B 1/I 1 Mohan Cooperative
    Industrial Area
Mathura Road, New Delhi 110 044
India

SAGE Ltd.
1 Oliver's Yard
55 City Road
London EC1Y 1SP
United Kingdom

SAGE Asia-Pacific Pte. Ltd.
33 Pekin Street #02-01
Far East Square
Singapore 048763

Printed in the United States of America.

Library of Congress Cataloging-in-Publication Data

Kryza, Kathleen.
Inspiring elementary learners: nurturing the whole child in a differentiated classroom/Kathleen Kryza, Alicia Duncan, S. Joy Stephens.
    p. cm.
Includes bibliographical references and index.
ISBN 978-1-4129-6064-9 (cloth
ISBN 978-1-4129-6065-6 (pbk.)

   1. Differentiated teaching staffs. 2. Individualized instruction. 3. Mixed ability grouping in education. 4. Education, Elementary. I. Duncan, Alicia. II. Stephens, S. Joy. III. Title.

LB1029.D55K788 2009
372.1102—dc22   2008030621

This book is printed on acid-free paper.

08   09   10   11   12   10   9   8   7   6   5   4   3   2   1

Acquisitions Editor:	Carol Chambers Collins
Editorial Assistant:	Brett Ory
Production Editor:	Eric Garner
Copy Editor:	Gretchen Treadwell
Typesetter:	C&M Digitals (P) Ltd.
Proofreader:	Theresa Kay
Indexer:	Molly Hall
Cover Designer:	Michael Dubowe
Graphic Designer:	Lisa Riley

Contents

List of Figures

Preface

To Our Colleagues,

Our decision to collaborate and write our first book, *Inspiring Secondary Learners*, came from our mutual passion and desire to inspire *all* students to honor themselves, honor other learners, and to become lifelong learners. So we wrote a book that showed teachers the "big picture" as well as step-by-step instructions for how to (1) nourish the hearts of students within a rich and diverse learning community, (2) open students' minds to the joy of learning, and thus (3) create inspired learners. But we realized we couldn't stop there, because our elementary colleagues were pleading for us to hurry and write a book for them as well. So here we are again, moving toward the same destination, but from a different path. (Funny, that's exactly what we want to teach you to do, help all students reach the same destination, but from different learning pathways.)

So, our journey continues on and we would like to invite you to come join us as we explore from the perspective of elementary learning. We are still on the path, not at the destination. And, to paraphrase Albert Camus, sometimes the journey itself is enough to fill one's soul. For us, this journey has become a passion and we feel compelled to share what we are discovering with you in this book. Even the process of writing these books has been a process of growth and developing new understandings. It has truly transformed how we view our work as educators. As a result, we are different teachers, we are deeper thinkers, and we are different neighbors, stewards, and humans.

As we travel on this journey, we are rethinking the way we teach, the way we view and speak to our students, the way we see our classrooms, and the way we interact with each other. It's more than a rethinking really; it is a shift in vision and focus. In this era of high-stakes testing, it is a journey that reminds us we are teaching *kids*, not curriculum.

You will notice the phrase, "The Whole Child," in the title of this book. In the Association for Supervision and Curriculum and Development (ASCD) *Report of the Commission on the Whole Child*, they note, "Our children deserve an education that emphasizes academic rigor as well as the essential 21st-century skills of critical thinking and creativity."

In Daniel Pink's book, *A Whole New Mind*, he and other economists are finding the emergence of a new age that they call the conceptual age. Pink purports that those who are angled to be the most successful in the coming age are those who can integrate skills beyond technical, analytical thinking but also see holistically, synthesize concepts, and perform other right-directed thinking.

Preparing our students for the conceptual age will mean teaching them to integrate both sides of their hemispheric process into a whole mind process. We are inspired by ASCD, Pink's call to action for preparing our society for the future, as well as other organizations such as the Bill and Melinda Gates Foundation and the George Lucas Educational Foundation who are all sharing the same message for educating our children for the future.

Through the creation of a differentiated classroom, we are developing classrooms that move beyond standardized test scores (a dominate left-brain process) to a balanced approach of teaching conceptual connections and finding deep meaning. The balance that is created in a differentiated classroom is at the very essence of integrating the process of right-directed and left-directed thinking to help students develop a whole mind.

So, what will you encounter as you journey through this book? You will take a peek into Inspiring Classrooms and Schools through Inspiring Snapshots that are interspersed throughout the book. These snapshots are based on actual classroom experiences and have been included to help you envision and create your own Inspiring Classroom. You will learn about the research and theories that support best methodologies for reaching elementary learners, as well as tried and true, practical and doable steps for translating theory into practice in your classroom. (Teachers who use the best methodologies for reaching the elementary learning brain are best preparing their students not only for tests, but also for life!) Using these step-by-step strategies, activities, lessons, and designs will relight the fire of learning in your students, help them discover why they love learning—and you can meet state standards at the same time.

But more importantly, we believe this journey will allow you to uncover or rediscover the gifts you have *always known about yourself.* You will recall the beliefs that led you into teaching, which may have been buried by years of frustration over a system that requires more and more from us. When you rekindle your beliefs, and give yourself permission to grow and teach using practices that inspire you, you will inspire others in ways yet to be revealed.

So come join us. Remember, it's a journey, not a destination, and the rewards will fill your soul!

—Kathleen, Alicia, and Joy

P.S. When we talk about diversity in this book, we are extending beyond cultural, linguistic, and academic diversity. Understanding diversity shows appreciation for the uniqueness of each individual.

Acknowledgments

As Sir Isaac Newton said, "I have seen further than most only because I have stood on the shoulders of giants." Now that's a new *perspective*. Our thinking for this book is based on the current educational research in metacognitive strategies, learning styles, multiple intelligences, differentiated instruction, constructivist thinking, brain research, and choice theory. We see ourselves as interpreters between the world of philosophy and the reality of the classroom. We would like to thank the great educational thinkers of today from whom we have learned so much about helping students grow as learners. We are indebted to William Glasser, Carol Ann Tomlinson, Patricia Wolfe, Eric Jensen, Lucy Calkins, Nancie Atwell, Howard Gardner, Thomas Armstrong, Susan Weinbrenner, David Sousa, and The National Research Council (for their wonderful book, *How People Learn*).

Corwin Press gratefully thanks the following peer reviewers for their contributions to this book:

Kristen Acquarelli
Director of Mathematics, retired
San Diego Unified School District
San Diego, CA

Roxie R. Ahlbrecht
Math Teacher Leader and Second Grade Classroom Teacher
Robert Frost Elementary, Sioux Falls Public 49-5
Sioux Falls, SD

Laura Porter
Educational Consultant
Research for Better Teaching
Sudbury, MA

About the Authors

Kathleen Kryza consults internationally for her company, Infinite Horizons, and also presents nationally for the Bureau of Education and Research (BER). Kathleen has more than twenty years experience in motivating and reaching children, educators, and others through her teaching, consulting, coaching, and writing. Her expertise is in working with students in special education, gifted education, alternative education, and multicultural education. She has a master's degree in special education and is an adjunct professor at University of Michigan Ann Arbor and Dearborn. Kathleen is also an active volunteer for the Challenge Day programs in Washtenaw County. She resides in Ann Arbor, Michigan, with her husband, Roger, and their "kids" Rennie (the dog) and Sasha (the cat).

Alicia Duncan is a consultant, program coordinator, and teacher trainer for the Waterford School District in Waterford, Michigan. She shares her expertise across the state of Michigan and throughout the nation in reaching and teaching English language learners, gifted students, culturally diverse learners, and inclusion students through differentiated instruction. She has a master's degree in ESL teaching methodology. She resides in Waterford, Michigan, with her husband, Noel, and their gifted (and challenging) feline companions, Henry and Harold.

S. Joy Stephens teaches two beautiful children (on a 24 hour basis!) to honor themselves as unique individuals. She has taught middle and high school students of all levels and abilities in differentiated science, math, and foreign language classrooms. She is a presenter and trainer in practical strategies for differentiating classrooms and inspiring students. She holds a master's degree in biology and resides outside of Memphis, Tennessee, with her husband, Mark, and two inspiring children, Alex and Susie.

1

Growing Lifelong Learners

If you change the way you look at things, the things you look at change.

—Wayne Dyer (2006)

A garden is a perfect place to receive inspiration. As we stroll through a garden, the colors, the textures, and the scents in the air all come together to create a beautiful community that feeds our soul. This garden community does not come together of its own will. It thrives because of the time, energy, and passion of a gardener. In a garden, there are many different plants all needing different things. Some of them are wilting and in need of basic nutrients, others are growing, but need a trellis to help them reach great heights. Some need to be moved to get more sunlight; others need to be put with similar plants to share common nutrients. Some plants thrive with little care. A gardener is an observer of his plants, watching carefully as each one grows, deciding what amount of sunlight, nutrients, and water each needs.

When we look at our responsibilities as teachers, we are much like a gardener. However, unlike most gardeners, we are not fortunate enough to get to choose only red roses to plant in our garden. We are given a landscape, if you will, of individuals with many unique gifts and many different needs. The beginning of our growing season might start out like this:

- Ms. Pica, the special education teacher, comes in and tells you that you have three special needs students in your class, one with Asperger syndrome, one learning disabled, and one with emotional problems. She hands you a to-do list of how to meet their academic needs.

- Jose joins your class from Ecuador. He barely speaks English and you have no information about his educational background.
- Tony and Brian incessantly wiggle in their seats and have difficulty focusing on written assignments.
- Then, there is Wenting, who slouches in her seat and refuses any attempt you make to connect with her.
- Oh yeah, and Noel is reading two grade levels ahead of the rest of the class.

So, Mistress Mary, how does your garden grow? Trying to nourish all these challenging plants might leave us feeling hopeless, but with an inspired vision, we can see beyond the rocks and the dirt, the thorns and the thistles—we see that beneath the surface lies a beauty that is waiting to be nurtured. What if we shifted our thinking from "this will never work" to "this is what we can become"? At the end of the first week of school, a teacher with an inspired vision would share something like this:

- Ms. Pica sure is a gift for me. I'm looking forward to our collaboration as we develop ways to meet Ronnie and Juanita's Individualized Education Plan (IEP) goals. Ronnie has Asperger syndrome but is already showing a natural ability with math, which will help our class go deeper with reasoning skills. Juanita is emotionally fragile, but with her great art skills, we've been able to create a lot of picture clues for Jose. I can see they are already gaining confidence in the strengths that they have uncovered this week.
- Jose, from Ecuador, has been bringing in artifacts from his home and helping us to understand more about his culture; seeing the similarities in our experiences is very powerful for all the kids. And, the kids are really having fun with the greetings and phrases he has been teaching us.
- Brian and Tony are wiggly worms but they are great "body smart" kids and have been showing us movements to learn vocabulary terms from our story this week.
- Now, Wenting has been harder to reach. But after discovering she is interested in music, she shared a beautiful song about reoccurring patterns with the class on Thursday. Her confidence surfaced and two kids came to her for help with next week's lesson.
- And that Noel, he is excited about looking for books with common themes to lead a book discussion group in the next unit.

So, we have a choice. We can choose to allow all these differences to be an obstacle to reaching and teaching our students. Or we can be joyfully curious, seeing the possibilities—the gifts—that each one brings not only to our teaching, but to our life.

This book came about because of our desire to help educators like ourselves nurture their own gifts as well as the gifts in each and every child. In our research for this second book, we stumbled across the writings of Dr. Wayne Dyer, an internationally renowned author and speaker in the area of self-development. He is the author of *Inspire: Our Ultimate Calling* (2006). To make teaching truly fulfilling for our students, as well as ourselves, we must teach from a place of inspiration, rather than motivation.

When we attempt to motivate another person (or ourselves), we are trying to get him or her to do something that is in *our* interest (behave a certain way, learn a certain process, spit back what we have poured in, for example). Motivation attempts to change a person through external forces. As we already know, motivational strategies are behavioral band-aids that lose their effectiveness over time. If we truly want to reach our students and enjoy our work, our efforts need to come from *inspiration*! Inspiration is a stirring of something deep within us all that longs to be fulfilled. It is tapping into the innate nature of our students and as well as ourselves. Only when we inspire our students do they become driven by their internal desire to learn, not by our external "motivating." Only when we feel inspired by our work can we see beyond the systemic trappings that can make us feel overwhelmed, to the gifts our profession has to offer us.

To paraphrase Pablo Casals, cellist and peace activist, why are we teaching our students that 2x2=4 and Paris is the capital of France when we should be teaching them that they are marvels who are capable of anything. The truth is, there should be a balance between inspiring students to discover who they are, encouraging them to find their unique talents, while also delivering important content.

One of the greatest needs of the human spirit is to be inspired and to inspire (Secretan, 2004). An inspired gardener knows that he cannot change the inherent nature of the flower. (He can't make a pink flower red and he can't make a sun-loving plant thrive in the shade.) He can only create an environment built upon a very strong foundation of good soil and nutrients, which allows each individual plant to flourish into their natural, inherent beauty. Similarly, an inspired teacher knows that she cannot change the inherent nature of her students. She can only create a learning environment where students' strengths are honored and they are allowed to flourish and share their gifts. Now, let's take a look at the foundations of an Inspiring Classroom, where those critical nutrients that allow the inner beauty of each child to grow are established.

FOUNDATIONS OF THE INSPIRING CLASSROOM

After numerous discussions, reflections, and clarifications, we have identified three foundations of an Inspiring Classroom:

1. An interdependent community based on honoring students' strengths.

2. Learners who are honored as individuals and inspired.

3. Lessons that are engaging and meaningful.

To help us see how the three essential foundations shift our classroom environment from an outward, motivating environment to an inward, Inspiring Classroom, let's take a step back and look at how these three foundations played a role in classrooms from the past.

For decades, our classrooms consisted of desks neatly arranged in rows. Students were quietly on task, each focused on the same assignment in preparation for the same assessment. In this teacher-controlled environment, there was little collaboration and little place for diversity of thinking or action. Was this an Inspiring Classroom? Not likely. What was missing?

1. Students worked primarily on their own and therefore had little opportunity to honor others for their abilities and contributions. So there was no appreciation for **community.**

2. Teachers did not consider how their students learned and students were not taught to value themselves as learners so they were not **honored and inspired learners.**

3. Lessons were not designed according to students' readiness, interests, or learning profiles so they were not **engaging and meaningful lessons.**

What followed were classrooms where students were tracked according to their readiness levels. In an attempt to provide all students with appropriately challenging curriculum, schools grouped pupils according to their perceived abilities, sometimes being pulled out of the classroom for random enrichment activities or grouped into remediation centers for repeated skill and drill practices. Tracking of students was typically based on standardized test scores and teacher recommendations. Teachers' recommendations were often influenced by student behavior; therefore, well-behaved students were placed in higher or gifted tracks while other, less teacher-pleasing students ended up in lower tracks. Once again this was not an Inspiring Classroom. Why?

1. Students were not encouraged to value all learners for their unique abilities and contributions and therefore it was not a **community.**

2. Instruction tried to match students' readiness, but there was no consideration made for their learning styles and interests so the students were not **honored and inspired learners.**

3. Since the pullout programs were often disconnected from the curriculum standards, lessons were not **engaging and meaningful.** The result of tracking was that struggling learners still struggled, while advanced learners continued to be superficially challenged.

Clearly, these prior attempts moved us in the direction of discovering what our students needed as learners. These past attempts were our best intentions based on what we knew at the time about the learning brain. What is so exciting about teaching today is that we now have a wealth of research on how the brain learns. This research offers us some very important information about the learning brain as it applies directly to our classroom instruction.

With this in mind, let's look at how our three foundations connect to what we now know about the learning brain. We know that each of our student's brains takes in and processes information differently, through varied contexts and patterns. We have learned that the brain is a social brain, and an emotional brain; it learns most effectively working with others in a safe, supportive environment. Also, we know that the brain learns best when the learning is relevant to the learner (Jensen, 1998). The brain research thus leads us to these three conclusions:

1. If the brain learns best in a safe, supportive environment, we must create a **community** of interdependent learners who respect, value, and learn from the diversity around them.

2. If each brain learns differently, then we must **honor** our students by getting to know them as learners and by keeping their needs in mind as we design our lessons. We must **inspire** our students to become individuals who know and value themselves as learners, and who assess their growth as learners.

3. If the brain requires relevance, we must inspire learners by designing **engaging and meaningful lessons** with clear learning targets that connect to the curriculum expectation and, most importantly, to their world.

These foundations, much like the essential elements a garden needs to flourish, create the opportunity for learning for all individuals. It cannot happen, though, without an inspired teacher who envisions possibilities and understands the gift she is to the classroom.

HONORING OUR ROLE AS TEACHERS

Why did we go into teaching? Not all of us entered into this profession out of our innate desire to inspire our students to be lifelong learners. Perhaps, you were from the generation for which teaching was one of the few options open to women. Perhaps, because of your love of baseball, you thought this a perfect outlet for your passion as a coach and teacher. Maybe this was a career that would be conducive to having a family. Maybe you were born knowing that teaching was your destiny. Maybe you weren't. That's okay. Honor yourself; honor your role as a teacher. Then be open to a moment when you realize that you have truly inspired a student. It is in that moment that you can consciously begin to create an Inspiring Classroom.

For the teacher in the Inspiring Elementary Classroom, there is always an aha! moment:

"I was sitting there with my third grade students, under a tree, independently reading on a lovely spring day. Because it was windy, my hair kept blowing into my face, and I kept brushing it away. When I asked a young man in my class to respond to a question, the boy moved his hand across his face just as I had moved my hand across my face. In that simple moment of him modeling my gesture, I realized with a jolt, 'This is a very powerful position.'" Aha!

"Mitchell would never do his assignments. In frustration one day, I took him out in the hall and I asked him, 'What can I do to get you to do this assignment?' Mitchell said he would be willing to draw his assignment.

In exasperation, I said, 'Okay!' Well, the next day, he brought in a poster he had drawn. It was beautiful. He was totally capable of processing the information I was teaching. I just wasn't giving him a choice about how to get it out. What he had to offer was never honored." Aha!

"I was twenty-five and after four years of subbing, a thankless job that nearly made me leave the profession altogether, I finally had my own classroom. As I stood in front of my class that first day, I looked out at all those beautiful faces, lives that I would touch, and the magnitude of my responsibility in shaping their young lives blew me away. At that moment my job shifted from a profession to a calling." Aha!

These teachers clearly received from their students the inspiration they needed to become teachers who inspire. A teacher in an Inspiring Classroom has the following core beliefs:

1. *All students can learn.* The preconceptions we have of our students tend to influence our behavior toward them, which in turn can affect our students' achievement. To dispel teachers' lounge rumors of how impossible it is to reach Ben or Susie or Jose, we must enter our classroom each and every day with the firm belief that all students can learn. Students believe in themselves as learners when our words and actions consistently reflect our belief in them.

2. *All students learn differently.* Inspiring teachers believe that "Fair is not everybody getting the same thing, fair is everybody getting what each needs to be successful." Practical classroom experience makes it obvious to all of us that each student brings his or her own set of interests, abilities, and motivations to learning. So why would we offer only one way to teach them? The key question we must ask ourselves is "Are my actions and choices providing each student with access to learning?"

3. *Learning occurs through risk taking and mistake making!* No one ever learned anything by playing it safe. It is when something is new and challenging that real learning occurs. If we want our students to be risk takers, we must be risk takers ourselves. Remember the old adage, "monkey see, monkey do." If our students see us as risk-taking teachers, they will be more willing to leave their own safety zone and take on their own learning risks! And, isn't it a good feeling to know that when we make mistakes as we grow our teaching practice, we are actually inspiring our students to be mistake makers and risk takers themselves?

4. *Students learn what teachers emphasize.* When we look at our students, what characteristics are they displaying in the classroom? Are they disorganized, controlling, apathetic, or impatient? Might they be seeing any of those *same* qualities in us? We must evaluate what we see in our students and then ask ourselves, what do *they* see in *us*? How can we expect them to be excited about learning if they can see that we are clearly not excited about teaching? To paraphrase Gandhi, we must be the change we want our students to be. When

we love what we do and are enthusiastic about learning, can there be any room for apathy in our students?

5. *Our greatest strengths are our greatest weaknesses.* We all bring special talents to the classroom that need to be used to inspire students. But have we ever considered that our greatest strength could also be our greatest weakness? We may have a great gift for managing a highly efficient classroom. However, this gift may be our greatest weakness when it comes to reaching students who are random, creative thinkers. Perhaps we have amazing energy and a commanding voice in the classroom. Yet, that gift may be an obstacle to connecting with the student who needs quiet processing time. We must continually remind ourselves that we are designing lessons for students who learn just like us, but *also* for students who learn very differently from us.

In the Inspiring Classroom, these core beliefs guide our actions and focus our intentions.

HONORING OUR FELLOW TEACHERS

Historically, there has been a tendency in our profession to teach in isolation of others. We come up with our own plans, keep our doors closed, and teach "our" kids and reflect alone on our practice. Yet, there is tremendous untapped potential to grow our teaching practice when we reach out and collaborate with our colleagues. (Two heads *really* are better than one!)

We honor others, honor their strengths and talents, when we invite them to collaborate with us. If we look around, we will see many opportunities to invite others to join us in this amazing journey. We can do the following:

- Honor teaching colleagues. Collaborating with them when writing lessons is a fun and powerful way to meet the needs of all learners creatively. We will design better lessons and have more fun designing them when we work with others.
- Honor learning specialists. Asking building experts for help with learners who have unique needs (e.g., special needs students, gifted students, English language learners) is a great way to brainstorm new strategies for reaching those unique learners.
- Honor outside experts. Honoring the opportunity to learn from experts by attending district and outside workshops opens up new ideas from outside our schools.
- Honor textbook authors. Many of today's textbooks offer great resources for adapting activities to meet the needs of all learners. Spending some time with that "pile of stuff" that comes with our textbooks, looking for key words like *adaptation, enrichment, adjustment,* etc., will give us further resources for reaching students.
- Honor the Internet community. There are many professional Web sites where teachers communicate and share ideas about how to help students. Don't forget to explore the plethora of lesson ideas that can be found online as well.

- Honor parents. Tapping into parents for information about what works at home gives us a bigger picture for understanding the student's needs.

As we honor ourselves as teachers and honor our colleagues, we must not forget one of the most important contributors in the learning experience—our students. Each and every day we have the opportunity to learn something from them.

HONORING OUR STUDENTS

A gardener closely watches and monitors his plants to determine what each one needs to thrive. With gardening log in hand and a detailed diary, he comes to know each plant so well that he can adjust his actions to meet their needs. When we get to know our students, we honor them. Collecting data about our students enables us to plan lessons that are meaningful and relevant to them. As we learn who they are, they learn who they are as learners. They are better able to grow their skills and confidence and have ownership over their learning. Honoring and knowing our students is not just an outward display of appreciation or respect, it is an underlying attitude that says, "I accept you, your spirit, everything about you. You are uniquely you and I want to know how to reach you." Much of Chapter 3 will be devoted to discovering ways to know and honor your students.

WHAT IS THE INSPIRING CLASSROOM?

The Inspiring Classroom is a place where we honor ourselves, where we honor our colleagues, and where we honor our students. It's a place where the love of teaching comes alive in every interaction, lesson, and activity, and is expressed as excitement and wonder. It's a place where we see who our students are and what they bring to the classroom community. It's a place of endless possibilities. For, as Dr. Wayne Dyer says in his book *Inspiration: Your Ultimate Calling,* "when you are inspired, your mind transcends limitation."

INSPIRING SNAPSHOT

An Inspiring School

The principal at Farms Elementary, Mr. Keenan, encourages and supports his staff in many ways. He leaves personal notes in mailboxes when teachers have contributed above and beyond. He stops in classrooms each day to ask students to do their personal best. On staff development days, he plans a wonderful lunch and shares success stories. The most inspiring day, however, is the day Mr. Keenan had the courage to let his teachers know that at Farms Elementary School, kids come first, not test scores.

After the usual lovely luncheon, he asked to have a brief talk with the staff. He began by explaining that a "Four Letter Word" had been used too much in the school this year. He personally apologized for that and said that things were going to change at Farms from now on. Mr. Keenan went on to explain that the "Four Letter Word" was NEAP, the name of the state test. He said he had placed too much emphasis on the test and he saw that this had made the Farms school climate less than inspiring. Noting that research shows that teaching for deep understanding with relevant meaning that connects to the students' lives is what really helps student perform better, not just on the test, but beyond the test, he said that from now on he and the staff were going to stay focused on putting kids first. They would learn and use best teaching practices so they could continue to make their school a place where kids *wanted* to come and learn. He then unveiled a hot pink piñata he had made with the word NEAP emblazoned on it. With baseball bat in hand, he invited Ms. Field, his assistant principal and unhappy enforcer of the NEAP rules, to come and smash the heck out of the piñata, which she did, with great gusto!

The staff, who had gathered around the piñata, acted accordingly and grabbed at the treats that spilled out. Each piece of the candy was wrapped with paper that coincided with special prizes he had attached to gift bags for each staff member.

Mr. Keenan's courage to act on his beliefs gave his staff permission to also do the right thing—focus on making their school a rigorous and *inspiring* place to learn.

2

The Inspiring Classroom

Theory Into Practice

I have seen further than most only because I have stood on the shoulders of giants.

—Sir Isaac Newton

When we began to write this book, our conversations focused predominantly on the *practices* we thought would help teachers reach, teach, and inspire their students. But as our conversations evolved, we realized it was that *beliefs* we held about learning had had the most powerful effect in our classrooms; this realization steered and guided our decisions about our instructional practices. After hours of talking, listening, and thinking, we distilled those beliefs into the three essential foundations of an Inspiring Classroom: (1) a community based on honoring diversity, (2) learners who are honored and inspired, and (3) lessons that are engaging and meaningful.

THREE FOUNDATIONS OF AN INSPIRING CLASSROOM

These three foundations grew from and are supported by key learning theories that impacted our beliefs and changed our practices. Figure 2.1

Figure 2.1   Foundations of an Inspiring Classroom

		FOUNDATIONS OF AN INSPIRING CLASSROOM		
CONNECTS TO:		*Chapter 3* **A Community Built Upon Honoring Diversity**	*Chapter 3* **Honored and Inspired Learners**	*Chapters 8–13* **Engaging and Meaningful Lessons**
KEY EDUCATIONAL THEORIES	**Choice Theory** Glasser	Focus is on building students' power *within* themselves, on learning *with* students, not teaching *at* them	Personal needs are recognized and responded to: relationships are built on a foundation of trust	Personal filters influence what we experience and how we understand Mastery learning
	Constructivist	Experiences allow for students to be willing and able to learn; positive classroom experience All ideas are valued	Empowerment; students discover principles themselves: students own the learning	Students create meaning using prior knowledge to construct own understanding
	Brain Research	The brain is a social brain, an emotional brain; it learns most effectively working with others in a safe, supportive community	Each brain takes in and processes information *differently*, through varied contests and patterns	The brain learns best when the learning is relevant to the learner
Foundation: High quality curriculum written around concepts, understandings, and knowledge, and designed to ensure maximum individual growth along with a sense of community. (Wiggins & McTighe, 1998)				

captures the connection between our three foundations for creating an Inspiring Classroom and the key learning theories. As you begin your journey toward creating your own Inspiring Classroom, know that the effectiveness of these three foundations is supported by a wealth of both research and practice. Our goal throughout the rest of this book is to guide you and provide a toolkit of doable, manageable classroom practices that will inspire your teaching and allow you to inspire your students.

If we reflect upon these foundational theories, it becomes obvious that one-size-fits-all practices don't work. Therefore, if we are to honor and inspire all learners in our classrooms, we need to find engaging and meaningful paths to differentiate our instruction and meet our district learning targets.

Think back over your past few weeks of teaching. Ask yourself the following questions:

- Have I set a tone in the room that respects and honors all learners? How do I know? What evidence can I provide to illustrate that I have honored my students?
- Is the physical environment in my classroom invigorating and student centered?

- Is there a sense of community in my classroom? Do students respect each other? Do they learn and grow together?
- Do I offer various ways for students to access the content I am teaching? What are those ways?
- Do I present new ideas and information to students in various ways?
- How do I allow students to process what I just taught them? Do they have a choice in how they get to process new learning?
- How do I check for understanding? Do I take into consideration that students show understanding in different ways?
- Reflecting on our answers to these questions, we should begin to get a picture of whether our teaching style and our beliefs are in alignment with the three foundations of the Inspiring Classroom. We should also notice the balance we offer in terms of routine and novelty in our classrooms.

FIVE ELEMENTS TO DIFFERENTIATE

The learning brain requires both novelty and routine (Sousa, 2000). We *must* build routine into our teaching day. The procedures we teach our students (how to enter and exit the classroom, work in groups, turn in papers, etc.) become the routines that allow our classrooms to flow smoothly, that create more time for us to teach effectively.

However, if we follow the same *teaching* pattern each day (read the book, do the questions or worksheet, take a quiz or test) chances are students are not going to look at us, eyes shining with wonder and enthusiasm, as they learn our subject. Teaching, using repetitive methods, does not honor our students' needs to access learning in a variety of ways. Routine teaching is guaranteed to make students lose their passion for learning!

To *nurture* students' passion for learning, there are five elements we can differentiate in our classroom instruction. Figure 2.2 and Figure 2.3 provide an overview of those elements.

It is important, in becoming inspiring teachers, that we note which of the elements we are already skilled at or are working toward developing, and which elements we most need to develop.

An easy framework to begin or extend our skills at honoring all learners is by designing our lessons using the *chunk, chew,* and *check* steps.

 Chunk: *New information is presented to the learner.* The brain learns best when it receives new information in small chunks. Because each brain perceives incoming information differently, we need to vary how we offer *chunks* of new learning.

 Chew: *The learner has to make sense of the information.* All brains have a unique way of connecting new information to what it already knows. Therefore, we need to offer students a variety of ways to *chew* on new information we have presented to them.

Check: *The teacher checks if the learner has processed the information.* We know that individuals possess unique talents and therefore demonstrate understanding in their own ways. We need to balance the ways we *check* for student understanding. Keeping the *chunk, chew,* and *check* framework in mind as we design our lessons helps us vary our teaching and offer better access to learning for all students in our classrooms. We also need to support differentiating by creating an environment and working with the content in ways that honor all learners.

Environment: *Tone and setting of the classroom.* The learning brain learns best in a safe environment. We need to work to build a community and an environment that respects all learners and offers them safe access to learning.

Content: *What we teach.* Our students come to us with different readiness levels and different interests. We need to teach to the same learning objectives, but vary the content based on the readiness levels or interests of our students.

Figure 2.2   Five Elements We Can Differentiate

Three Steps of Every Lesson			The Fundamentals	
1. Input	2. Process	3. Output		
Information In		Info Out	The Information	Environment

Taking in new chunks of information through
 	
☐ Seeing the information in charts/graphs/ notes
 	
☐ Reading information from books, magazines, online
 	
☐ Hearing the information through lecture/ discussions
 	
☐ Manipulating, doing, or building to gain the information
	Making sense of new of information by
	
	☐ Writing to help students connect the new information
	
	☐ Drawing pictures/ concept maps to connect the new information
	
	☐ Talking or listening to connect the new information
	
	☐ Doing, manipulating, or building to connect the new information
		Showing understanding and knowledge of information by
		
		☐ Selecting from various problems in a textbook to show students' understanding
		
		☐ Choosing different projects that show understanding of what is learned according to individual strengths:
		    Write a
		        poem
		    Sing a song
			☐ Reading different texts that are easier/ harder
			
			☐ Using alternative methods (video, tapes, experiments, computers) at easier or harder levels
			
			☐ Exploring information through different levels of questioning
			
			☐ Exploring information through varying levels of depth and complexity
				Effective Atmosphere
				
				☐ Students' strengths are acknowledged and used to help them grow and learn
				
				☐ Risk taking and mistake making are encouraged
				
				☐ The relationships within the learning community are focused on helping one another grow
				
				Physical Setting
				
				☐ The energy level of the learning environment changes depending on the goal/task; sometimes relaxed focused learning, sometimes enthusiastic investigations
				
				☐ The lighting, seating, temperature, and sounds

Chunk	**Chew**	**Check**		

(Continued)

Figure 2.2 (Continued)

Three Steps of Every Lesson			The Fundamentals	
1. Input	**2. Process**	**3. Output**		
Information In		*Info Out*	**The Information**	**Environment**
		Build a project Make a video ☐ Showing what is learned through projects of varying difficulty based on students' readiness	☐ Exploring information through personal interests	in the environment change to meet various needs on various days ☐ The physical location for learning changes according to the outcome/goal ☐ Students work with varied groupings depending on the learning goal ☐ Student movement and material management supports student independence; they know what to do without asking
Chunk	**Chew**	**Check**		

This overview of the three foundations and five elements of the Inspiring Classroom gives us a framework— a schema—to guide our thinking. Throughout the rest of this book, we offer concrete and practical strategies for creating the Inspiring Classroom. Remember, we must be guided *first* by our beliefs. When we teach from our beliefs, the practices will follow.

Figure 2.3   Five Elements We Can Differentiate

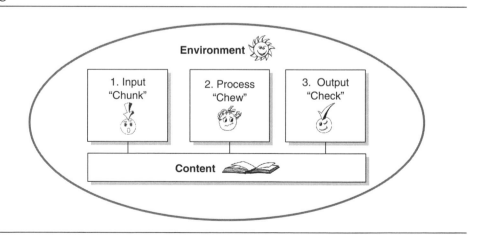

3

Building Community, Honoring Individuals

You won't help shoots grow by yanking on them.

—Chinese Proverb

How often have we felt we were yanking information out of our students? Yanking them along a road of learning that we thought was best for them? Yanking them in the direction of state standards and curriculum targets? How soon our arms wear out from continuous yanking as the weight of their resistance grows. Instead of yanking our students, let's focus on nurturing them from the inside by honoring their intrinsic gifts, their uniqueness, so that, as they learn our content in meaningful ways, they grow into lifelong learners.

And yes, they are all very different learners, with different skills, different backgrounds, and different needs. This diversity, both academic and cultural, presents us with two options. One, we can recognize that our students are all different, then continue with the one-size-fits-all teaching we've always done—like giving the same nutrients to every plant. Or, we can recognize and respond to those differences by saying to our students, "Your needs are unique. Help me find the right combination of nutrients, soil, and water that will help you to understand and grow as a learner."

In the Inspired Classroom, we send very clear messages with our words and actions:

"You are free to be you and learn in ways that work for you."

"You are free to try, to make mistakes, to grow, to become."

"Your ideas and talents are welcome here. They are needed and valued here."

"Everything you have is enough. We will all grow together and learn together."

"You are an integral part of this community, along with everyone else in this room."

These messages help us invent a world of inspiring possibilities in our classrooms. In this chapter, we will look at the first two of the three foundations of an inspiring classroom, building an interdependent community and honoring and inspiring individual learners.

BUILDING COMMUNITY: HELPING STUDENTS SEE THE VALUE OF OTHERS

As elementary learners enter our classes each year, it is common to see their excitement for what is to come. "Who will be my teacher? When will we have recess? I wonder what exciting things I will learn in school?" There is also much apprehension in young children. "Who will sit next to me? Will my teacher like me?" (And sadly, for some) "Will I get something to eat?" Our students may be leaving the comfort of home and family, insecure about what their days may be like. Perhaps they are searching for the comfort, attention, and sense of belonging that they are not getting elsewhere. In either situation or somewhere in between, it is essential to create an interdependent community where students feel safe to grow and learn, question and experiment, overcome failure and enjoy success.

The chart in Figure 3.1 represents the steps to creating a safe community from an Inspiring Classroom.

Figure 3.1   Steps to Creating a Classroom Community

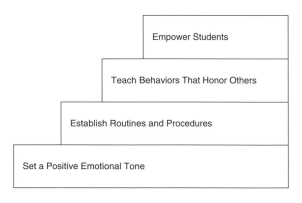

Empower Students
Teach Behaviors That Honor Others
Establish Routines and Procedures
Set a Positive Emotional Tone

Let's take a look at what each step would look like and sound like in your classroom, along with some practical activities to help you get started.

We must first create a **positive emotional tone** and message in our classroom. We want our students to feel welcomed by the learning environment. We want to create a space for our students where they feel safe making mistakes, safe being different, safe knowing they are accepted without condition. An Inspiring Classroom has a positive emotional tone that builds and supports community. It may *look* something like this:

- Use affirmation posters and bulletin boards. Students will know exactly what is important to us when our core beliefs are clearly defined and visible for all to see. Two messages that are essential to have posted in our classrooms are "This is a risk-taking and mistake-making classroom" and "Fair is not everyone getting the same thing; fair is everyone getting what they need to be successful." When we post these beliefs and live by them, we provide students with a powerful reminder that their needs are honored and that we are in the learning process together, mistakes and all!

SOURCE: Photos courtesy of Tammy Bosom and Deborah Moran, fourth grade teachers.

- Model honoring and inspiring behaviors. Robert Fulghum once said, "Don't worry that children never listen to you; worry that they are always watching you." Our students look to see if we are walking the walk of the messages we have posted on our walls. Can they see that we enjoy what we are doing? (That's inspiration!) Do they see how we honor the gifts of others? Do our words celebrate the contributions of all? (That's honoring!)

- Read, discuss, and display literature on topics of belonging, community, working together, and honoring differences in others. (See Resources for literature suggestions.)

- Set up a "Peace Corner" in your room. Here, students can come together and discuss problems they are having with other students. Through modeling and scaffolding, teach them the steps for conflict resolution. Have prompts in the corner to guide their discussions. The Peace Corner can also be used as a quiet place for students who need to calm down or destress. Include stuffed animals, squeeze toys, perhaps a soothing CD for them to listen to in this space.

- Provide materials and make them accessible to all. It may seem like a small thing, but have materials available for all means of learning and exploration (paint, colors, paper, manipulatives, etc.). Giving students access to materials reinforces the message of acceptance and promotes independence by saying, "This is *your* learning community and I trust that you will use what you need to help you learn."

- Create a classroom theme that speaks to your message such as, "I'm glad we're all different, aren't you?" or "*You* matter. Together we *all* matter." Themes create a sense of belonging, giving a class something in common to help them feel connected to one another. They also provide students with a frame of reference when learning new social skills, behaviors, and norms. (See Resources for a list of theme ideas.)

With younger children, activities that provide an analogy or frame of understanding for what community feels like are especially valuable. An Inspiring Classroom with a positive emotional tone that builds community may do an activity something like Figure 3.2:

Figure 3.2   Example of Community Building Activity

The Crayon Box That Talked

Grade: Kindergarten

Objective: Teaching students to appreciate others' differences. (Meets social studies and language arts standards.)

1. Discuss with the students what "different" means and what "same" means. Write their ideas on the board or chart.

2. Read *The Crayon Box That Talked*, by Shane Derolf. Ask the kids to think about what color crayon they would be and why they would be that color. What would they say?

3. After reading the story, have a few students share what color they would be and why and what would they say to the other crayons in the box.

4. Talk about personal space issues. How is sharing a box with other crayons like sharing space lying on the reading rug or sitting down at circle time? What is teamwork and why is it important?

5. Hand out black sheets of construction paper and pieces of colored chalk. Have the students draw the crayon they would be. Spray the drawing with hairspray to keep it from smearing.

SOURCE: Created by Brandie Taulliee, Whitmore Lake Elementary.

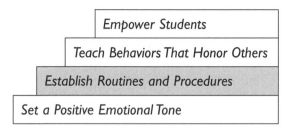

Empower Students

Teach Behaviors That Honor Others

Establish Routines and Procedures

Set a Positive Emotional Tone

Second, we create a deeper sense of community by **creating predictable routines and procedures**. When students are secure in how the classroom functions, they are able to take risks, make mistakes, and learn together and readily welcome a challenge or new situation. We help our classrooms function as a community by establishing procedures for the following:

- *Routines for classroom management.* The learning brain needs routine and predictability. When we establish routines, we are nurturing the students' capacity to work as a community. These strategies must be taught explicitly for young ones; then they must be modeled and practiced daily until there is no thought to what is supposed to happen next. Students are focused on the learning task at hand with no thought of "What do I do now?" We create community when we teach them routines such as . . .
  o How to enter and exit the room
  o Where and when to turn in papers
  o How and whom to ask for help ("See three before me")
  o How to transition from traditional seating arrangements into group arrangements
  o Where to go for supplies and materials
  o Activities for early finishers (See Resources for anchor activity ideas.)
- *Routines for problem solving—class meetings.* Class meetings are a time when students are systemically involved in problem solving and constructive decision making as a group. By establishing class meetings, we are developing a climate of respect and trust between students. Class meetings offer opportunities for the following:
  o Mutual establishment of classroom norms. From various perspectives and backgrounds, students work together to develop norms of behavior that are embraced in the classroom. In lieu of having the teacher establish the classroom routines for the classroom, the students are responsible for establishing procedures they feel will facilitate their learning and make their classroom functional for everybody.
  o Celebrating successes! What has been working? Where are we heading as a group? What progress have we made? How are individuals contributing their talents for the benefit of the group?

o Neutralizing tensions. If classroom problems arise such as cheating, bullying, or teasing, class meetings offer a place where groups can work on strategies and activities that promote positive communication, problem solving skills, and the redirecting of negative energy.

- *Routines for working collaboratively.* Grouping is a powerful tool for maintaining a well-functioning classroom and for deepening student thinking. For groups to run effectively, students must have established roles and responsibilities. This gives each student a purpose and direction; they *know* they are an integral part of the community and their contribution is valued. Some ways to help groups work well together are
  o Appointing jobs for each group member in a group. (Possible jobs: Leader, Recorder, Time Keeper, Teacher Getter, Positive Thinker, Organizer.)
  o Brainstorming with students to develop expectations for working productively as a group. (Possible Expectations: On Task, Sharing Ideas, Cooperating, Using Time Wisely.)
  o Creating a rubric of criteria, and asking each group to assess themselves at the end of each group work session. (See Resources for a group rubric template.) Go around the room and agree or disagree with groups' self-assessment. You can include the group assessment as part of the grade for the project.
  o Providing the class with feedback such as, "I really liked how DaShone's group was able to work through some of the problems the members were having and how the group was able to get back on track." or "I noticed some groups have members who are not clear on their responsibilities. Can we offer them some suggestions for solving that problem?"

| Empower Students |
| Teach Behaviors That Honor Others |
| Establish Routines and Procedures |
| Set a Positive Emotional Tone |

After setting the tone and establishing routines and procedures, we can teach behaviors that **honor** each other's gifts, talents, and differences. The classroom of today is different than the classroom of forty years ago. We can no longer assume that kids come to us knowing how to treat others respectfully, or even how to recognize and communicate their feelings and emotions. Honoring individuals in the classroom community may look something like this and is illustrated further with examples in Figures 3.3 and 3.4:

- Provide positive examples of how to effectively communicate with each other through teacher-led examples, role plays, posters, kindness boards, etc. We can model kindness phrases used to support others' ideas and work such as "Shea, I love how you used your strength in art to illustrate . . . " "Jackson, I agree with your ideas about . . . " Students will copy our language so we need to look for moments when they are incorporating effective communication into their speech.
- Incorporate activities, which focus on qualities of a community, into weekly routines. For example, one day a week we can discuss and reinforce the characteristics of a good community. (For example, on Wednesdays the class could work on building a community identity by discussing who they are a group, "We Are Wednesdays!") The

class can focus on characteristics such as respect, honor, trustworthiness, cooperation, fairness, dealing with feelings, appreciating ourselves, etc. On these days students can discuss, role play, brainstorm, read books, or problem solve issues related to quality communities.

- Create student designed bulletin boards where students can celebrate other students' strengths each week. Some themes could include "How Jaime contributes to our class"; "What we've learned from Dave"; or "What I admire about Rebecca." Make sure all students are acknowledged and receive feedback over a period of time.
- Conduct team-building activities. Facilitate activities where teams work to put together a puzzle without speaking, construct a model, send a message using art, create a dance that represents the class theme, etc. Afterwards, students should self-assess the group, reflecting upon what worked and didn't work and how they can work together better next time.
- Help students see the value that others bring by doing activities such as those in Figures 3.3 and 3.4.

Figure 3.3   Example of Activity to Honor Individual Gifts

I'm Gonna Like Me!

Grade: Kindergarten

Objective: Appreciating ourselves and others

Read Jamie Lee Curtis's *I'm Gonna Like Me!*

After reading, have students create pictures of themselves (you can let them use different mediums if you like—crayons, paint, chalk). Students write and/or explain "Why I like Me!"

Summarize the sharing by helping students understand that everyone brings something positive to the group.

SOURCE: Created by Andrea Gustafson, Whitmore Lake Elementary.

Figure 3.4   Example of Activity to Honor Individual Gifts

How Does Your Garden Grow?

Grade: Fourth

Objective: Nurture gifts of ourselves, honor gifts of others.

Read *Ms. Spitzer's Garden*, by Edith Pattou. After reading, have students create pictures of themselves as something from the garden. Next to the picture, students list the tools they already have as learners and what tools they need to bloom. On the back of the picture, students describe why they are like the plant/flower/tool they chose to draw.

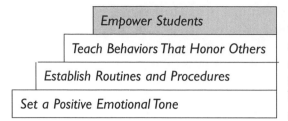

Empower Students

Teach Behaviors That Honor Others

Establish Routines and Procedures

Set a Positive Emotional Tone

With each of these community building steps, we are increasing students' empowerment and accountability for their own growth and the success of the community. What is more inspiring than someone saying "Here, you know what to do, I believe in your skills, go ahead and figure things out yourself or with your learning colleagues and know that if you have a problem, I'm here to help"?

In a community where students are empowered and accountable, you might see this:

- groups of students teaching and learning from each other
- routines and procedures led by students
- discussion and debate used for problem solving in group settings
- independent movement between assigned tasks and free choice anchor activities
- students supporting and reminding each other of appropriate classroom behaviors and work habits

Honoring our students and teaching them to thrive and see their place in diverse learning communities helps prepare our students for the future. Students who see themselves as contributing members of a classroom community will be prepared to enter the global community knowing they have their own unique talents to offer the world. They will also honor and respect that others have their place in the global community of the twenty-first century.

However, just as building a sports team, jumpstarting a business from scratch, and rearing children, nurturing a thriving community takes much time, energy, patience, and consistency, but the rewards are well worth the investment!

HONORING INDIVIDUALS: HELPING STUDENTS SEE THE VALUE IN THEMSELVES

Without an understanding of the unique meanings existing for the individual, the problems of helping him effectively are almost insurmountable.

—Arthur Combs

Students who are part of a nurturing community feel safe to take risks and grow as learners. In an Inspiring Classroom, we seek to uncover the talents of individual students—honoring who they are as learners, helping them understand how they learn, and how to use their strengths to help them be successful. First, we gather data about our students. Then we *use* that data to honor individual strengths and guide our instruction. See Figure 3.5 for information to collect about your students.

It is important to start with small steps as you begin to gather data about your students. Choose one way to gather data that you feel will

Figure 3.5 Collecting Data About Students

Data:	What It Is:	How to Collect:	Use It for:
Academic scores	Grades, standardized tests, pretests	Student records, formal and informal observations, test scores	Working with students by readiness levels
Learning preferences	Preferences students have regarding their learning environment	Learning preference surveys, student interviews, journaling prompts, discussions	Changing the physical environment to offer choices for how students work—on the floor, walking around, near a window, soft music playing, etc.
Learning styles	The way in which a student chunks, chews, and checks new information	Multiple Intelligences surveys, Sternberg's Intelligences surveys, Learning Style surveys, kid watching	Inform instruction to adapt to varying learning styles, grouping students by similar or varied learning styles, offering assignment choices with specific learning styles in mind
Interest inventories	Noting students' general interests, attitudes they have about subject areas, or content specific interests	Quick writes or quick "draws," general and content specific interest surveys, class surveys, letters to the teacher, classroom discussions	Grouping students with similar interests, prime new learning by making connections to their interests, offering choices based on their interests

most benefit you and what you want to know about your students. The earlier in the year you collect data, the sooner you will know your students and can begin to make accommodations and design lessons that honor their learning differences.

After gathering the data, however, it must be used! Instead of having a pile of surveys on the back desk or a folder in the back of the file cabinet, use the data to honor each individual and their unique needs. Then, refer to the data often as a tool for building community; drawing attention to the strengths of individuals makes everyone see that they "bring something to the table" and that they are all truly in this together.

Following are three examples of how teachers found user-friendly formats for gathering and *using* data about their students.

*Ms. Santos, a kindergarten teacher, simply used focused **kid watching**. During center time and independent exploration during the first two weeks of school, with clipboard in hand, she made the observations in Figure 3.6.*

Mrs. Santos has compiled her data in one easily accessible place. She refers to it frequently during lesson planning and in preparation for one-on-one time with the students (see Figure 3.6). This sheet serves as a reminder that Jonah needs strategies for challenging himself and Macie needs more opportunities to demonstrate her strengths in a group.

Figure 3.6   Excerpt From Focused Observation

Student	Work Habits	Learning Profiles and Strengths	Learning Challenges	I can honor his/her learning needs by trying to:
Macie	Keeps to herself	Is focused; Seems comfortable with own thoughts; Loves art; Self-smart	Doesn't participate in groups	Recognize her strengths; Group her with others who are weaker in art, allowing her strengths to be an integral part of the project
Hunter	Is full of energy and bounces around	Tries to work but shifts focus often; Enthusiastic; Loves learning; Full of ideas	Lacks confidence in his ideas	Use a timer for time on task to build stamina; Help him reflect on his growth to build confidence
Jonah	Gets frustrated with "menial" tasks	Finishes work quickly and thoroughly; Confident in his abilities; Perceptive!	Does not communicate reasons for his frustrations	Tier assignments to challenge him more; Teach him strategies for challenging himself

*Mr. Waltzman used **tick marks** to collect data about the learning preferences of his second graders. He compiled the data from each survey onto one survey that he laminated and keeps close at hand for reference.*

He was surprised to find out that twelve of his sixteen students preferred to work on the floor as opposed to sitting at the tables (see Figure 3.7). Against his better judgment, he allowed them to do so and was surprised to find that these students got their work done much more effectively in this

Figure 3.7   Sample Survey: Environmental Learning Preferences

prone position! Mr. Waltzman also noted that five of his students liked a little noise when it came to "quiet processing" time. He grouped them together in one corner with some background music during review time and saw an immediate shift in attitude toward their work and performance.

Ms. Keller, a fifth grade teacher, created a **learning profile system** *for better understanding her students by using 4 × 6 index cards. She gathers several pieces of data throughout the first days of school. After students complete a survey she has them summarize their findings on a 4 × 6 card. She then collects the cards and begins to add her own observations. Teachers of younger students may need to transfer the data onto the cards themselves, but the effort is well worth it. Mrs. Keller comments, "You know, it's sort of a pain to do the surveys and gather the data, but I now know about my students in September what I used to not know about them until April."*

After looking at the vocabulary for the social studies unit, Ms. Keller felt that students would understand the vocabulary most effectively if they were placed with students of the same multiple intelligence. Pulling out her data index cards (see Figure 3.8) the evening before class, she was able to arrange students quickly into art smart, word smart, body smart, and music smart groups. Students worked with others of the same intelligence strength to draw words, create word clues, do word charades, and compose word songs or rhythms. Students then shared their creations with others. Students, who work with others of the same learning strength, begin to internalize the learning and study skills that work best for them. Ms. Keller used the cards again to group students for a multimedia research project. She recognized that, this time, the final product would be more creative if students worked with others who had *different* learning styles and strengths.

Figure 3.8   Data Index Card

Learning Styles	Multiple Intelligences
Modality	
Interests / Hobbies	
(Student's name on back of card)	
Math Score	Environmental Learning Preferences
Reading Score	

How we gather information to better know our students varies from early elementary to later elementary. In K–2, we can use simple word prompts and pictures to find out more about our learners. In Grades 3–5, students can read scenarios and complete traditional surveys. Just as our three different teachers at three different points in their professional growth used three different ways to gather data, each of them understands the importance of getting to know their students and using that knowledge to create an Inspiring Classroom.

Building community and honoring learners are the first two foundations in establishing an inspiring classroom. These essential foundations are the underpinnings that allow us to efficiently and effectively teach in ways that are meaningful and engaging to all our students. The rest of our book is devoted to showing how to build the third foundation, Teaching for Meaning.

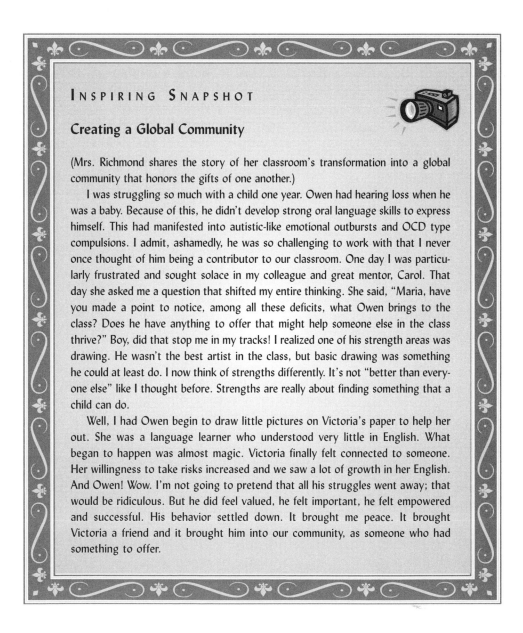

INSPIRING SNAPSHOT

Creating a Global Community

(Mrs. Richmond shares the story of her classroom's transformation into a global community that honors the gifts of one another.)

I was struggling so much with a child one year. Owen had hearing loss when he was a baby. Because of this, he didn't develop strong oral language skills to express himself. This had manifested into autistic-like emotional outbursts and OCD type compulsions. I admit, ashamedly, he was so challenging to work with that I never once thought of him being a contributor to our classroom. One day I was particularly frustrated and sought solace in my colleague and great mentor, Carol. That day she asked me a question that shifted my entire thinking. She said, "Maria, have you made a point to notice, among all these deficits, what Owen brings to the class? Does he have anything to offer that might help someone else in the class thrive?" Boy, did that stop me in my tracks! I realized one of his strength areas was drawing. He wasn't the best artist in the class, but basic drawing was something he could at least do. I now think of strengths differently. It's not "better than everyone else" like I thought before. Strengths are really about finding something that a child can do.

Well, I had Owen begin to draw little pictures on Victoria's paper to help her out. She was a language learner who understood very little in English. What began to happen was almost magic. Victoria finally felt connected to someone. Her willingness to take risks increased and we saw a lot of growth in her English. And Owen! Wow. I'm not going to pretend that all his struggles went away; that would be ridiculous. But he did feel valued, he felt important, he felt empowered and successful. His behavior settled down. It brought me peace. It brought Victoria a friend and it brought him into our community, as someone who had something to offer.

4

Apprenticeship Learning

Nurturing Lifelong Learners

Mentors and apprentices are partners in an ancient human dance and one of teaching's great rewards is the daily chance it gives us to get back on the dance floor. It is the dance of spiraling generations in which the old empower the young with their experience and the young empower the old with new life, reweaving the fabric of the human community as they touch and turn.

—Parker Palmer

Imagine teaching children how to ride their bicycles by having them watch us ride bikes, then giving a quiz on the parts of a bike and bike safety—then expecting them to go out and ride a bike. Would this method easily create expert and independent bike riders? No way! Instead, we teach children to ride bikes by offering them experiences in a progression toward independence. They begin by riding behind us on our bikes. We let them experience the freedom and fun as they join with us in this experience. Then we get them their first bike, a tricycle, which allows them to easily and successfully experience that first feeling of speed, momentum, and even fear that comes with freedom. When we sense they are ready for the next step, usually when they begin nagging us, we raise the bar of the challenge by getting them their first two-wheeler. (With training wheels, of course!)

Only when we see that they are ready for the final step do we take the training wheels off and let them have a go at the real thing. We stay very close to them during this process. We encourage all approximations of riding the bike, and help them keep going when the going gets tough. Then, as their skills progress, we let them go because we want them to experience that feeling of accomplishment that we, ourselves, remember so well. When we teach our children to ride bikes, we apprentice them into the skill of bicycling. We model and scaffold our bike-riding instruction. We know that children come to this skill at their own pace and in their own time. Ultimately, we know that if we let them practice, practice, practice under safe and nurturing conditions, they will know the sweet freedom of riding on their own.

MAINTAINING A BALANCE

The successful teacher, who prepares students for life in and outside of school, approaches teaching with this same apprenticeship model in mind. Teaching this way involves a balanced approach of both traditional teaching methods and differentiated teaching methods. There *are* skills and information we need to teach our students directly and explicitly. However, explicit teaching must be balanced with implicit learning experiences that allow students to own and have mastery of their learning.

In Figure 4.1, you will see the teaching methods listed under "Traditional Teaching." These will help students develop the skills they need to pass classes and obtain degrees. However, it is the teaching methods listed under "Differentiated Teaching" that will help students function independently and manage their lives on a day-to-day basis.

Figure 4.1   A Comparison of Traditional and Differentiated Teaching

Traditional Teaching	Differentiated Teaching
Teacher directed learning	Student created learning
Teacher choice	Student choice
Test taking skills	Products as assessment
Teacher feedback	Ongoing student self-assessment
Standards	Understandings
Teacher established criteria	Constructivist
Rote learning	Active learning
Explicit teaching	Implicit teaching
Learning alone	Learning with a community
Following directions	Creating plans
Listening	Discussing
Teacher generated questions	Student generated inquiry
Whole group instruction	Small group instruction for a variety of purposes (*readiness, special needs adaptations, interests, learning styles*)

As an example of why our students need to develop both sets of skills, let's reflect on the path we took to become educators. We needed success with traditional methods to obtain a university degree in education and pass state certification exams. However, the skills we need to be a truly effective teacher are much more complex. Our day-to-day success in the classroom requires differentiated skills such as multitasking, reflecting on our day's work, and creating plans for improving our teaching. Reading about these skills or taking a test does not develop these skills. These skills come from working with mentor teachers, collaborating with colleagues, teaching on our own, and reflecting on our teaching. *Both* the traditional learning and the life experiences create the balance needed for us to succeed in our work.

There is a time for traditional interactions with our students in which we are teachers and they are the learners. Eventually, however, if students are to take charge of their learning, our interactions need to shift to the mentor/ apprentice model. We need to teach explicitly, then model and scaffold the traditional skills we want students to eventually own. Figure 4.2 illustrates and offers examples of the shift from traditional to differentiated interactions.

If our goal is to have students who can ask questions and construct meaning from investigations or texts, we must build those skills. We cannot assume that all students will master the skills of independent learning to the same degree, just as we would not assume that every five-year-old has equivalent bike riding skills! Therefore, to move our students toward independence, our interactions must

> *Insanity is doing the same things over and over again and expecting different results.*
>
> —Einstein

Figure 4.2   Stages: Moving Toward Independence

Traditional Interactions Giving Explicit Instruction	Scaffolded Interactions Developing Vital Know-How	Differentiated Interactions Growing Student Independence
➤ Give information ➤ Teach and show ➤ Help students know or understand	➤ Conference and question ➤ Mentor and apprentice ➤ Help students own and apply independently	➤ Generate questions from students ➤ Prompt students to teach other students ➤ Develop student ownership and automatic application
• Teach the components of a persuasive essay • Explain the order of operations • Tell students about key historical figures and dates • Give directions for completing a lab, project, or report	• Model and generate persuasive writing together • Demonstrate using the order of operations • Involve student role play and discussion of events from history • Conference with students about their progress	• Teach students to use persuasion in real life applications • Create student-generated story problems/answer keys for order of operations problems • Use information from history to understand the world today • Ask students to make a plan for completing a project

move along a continuum. When students have no experience or knowledge, we must explicitly teach them the information. Next, we must help students practice the skills—the vital know-hows—that they need to become self-sufficient. Here, we offer supportive coaching while students attempt tasks on their own. Finally, we need to let go and *expect* students to be able to work on their own. We remain present to offer assistance when problems arise. As students move from the early elementary grades to upper elementary, teachers should continue to spiral and deepen students' skills. In fact, the modeling and scaffolding and eventual ownership of these skills does not stop in the elementary grades, but needs to be taught in the middle school and high school years as well.

Intelligence is not a matter of what you know; it's a matter of what you do when you don't know.

Below are descriptions of the most important five vital "know-hows" that lifelong learners need. Following the descriptions are the teaching methods that work most effectively in helping students develop those vital know-hows into lifelong learning tools. After that we have included some strategies for teaching the vital know-hows.

VITAL KNOW-HOWS FOR STUDENT SUCCESS

Vital Know-How #1: Reflective Learning

Definition: Reflective learning, or metacognition, is thinking about one's own thinking. Students who use reflective learning have a plan of action for what to do when they don't know.

Relevance: Learners who are self-reflective check to see if they are making sense of what they are learning, they assess what they know and still need to learn, and they reflect on what worked and what needs improving.

Ownership: Learners who are taught to be self-reflective increase the degree to which they are able to transfer their learning to new settings.

Vital Know-How #2: Discussion/Discourse

Definition: Discourse is the use of student-led conversations in order to deepen understanding. Learners take turns listening while other students verbally work through concepts and justify ideas.

Relevance: Learners who engage in discourse learn to listen to others, think deeply about their own ideas, and communicate effectively.

Ownership: Students who have skills in discourse can deepen their own understanding by constructing new meaning through conversations. They will be prepared to work collaboratively in the class and beyond.

Vital Know-How #3: Read/Write for Understanding

Definition: Strategic reading and writing skills are tools people use for processing and communicating understanding.

Relevance: Learners who have a toolkit of strategies for reading and writing are able to process and communicate more effectively in all subject areas. These skills need to be taught in all subject areas and grade levels (Biancarosa & Snow, 2004).

Ownership: Learners who read to understand are able to do the following:

- visualize what they are reading about
- sort important from interesting information
- ask good questions
- make connections between ideas
- recall what they have read
- evaluate and analyze new understandings
- self-monitor and adjust their thinking
- make inferences beyond the text

Learners who can write for understanding can do the following:

- take effective notes
- reflect on their understanding in logs or journals
- organize their thoughts into coherent written ideas
- write to learn, inform, persuade, and describe
- communicate their thoughts in a variety of writing genres

Vital Know-How #4: Inquiry/Research

Definition: Inquiry occurs when students ask thoughtful questions and determine ways to find answers to their questions.

Relevance: Learners who conduct long- or short-term research based on their own questions are able to search for answers, discover more, build knowledge, synthesize their thinking, and develop new insights.

Ownership: Learners who are involved in inquiry learn skills for answering their own questions and thus become more curious and engaged in their own learning.

Vital Know-How #5: Collaborative or Cooperative Learning

Definition: Collaborative learning is when students work effectively together on projects or tasks.

Relevance: The brain is a social brain and learns more effectively in a learning community than in isolation. (Two heads are better than one.)

Ownership: Students who learn the skills of collaboration will be able to work more effectively with others. This ability will help them not only in school but also in their personal relationships, in their careers, and in their communities.

HOW TO TEACH THE VITAL KNOW-HOWS

To effectively apprentice students into owning these vital know-hows, we need to teach them through modeling/ think alouds, explicit instruction, and scaffolding. Below is an explanation of each of these techniques, along with ideas for how to use them in your classroom.

When you plant lettuce, if it does not grow well, you don't blame the lettuce. You look into the reasons it is not doing well. It may need fertilizer, or more water, or less sun. You never blame the lettuce.

—Thich Nhat Hanh

Modeling/Think Alouds

What It Is

- You, the teacher, model aloud the metacognitive processes used for struggling with learning and for getting unstuck.
- When modeling thinking about your learning, be sure to talk through how you monitor and adjust your thinking.
- As students catch on to the idea of thinking aloud, have them talk through and share their processing.
- Mental modeling helps students see how good learners comprehend what they are reading, develop writing ideas, solve problems, etc.

How-To

- Determine the skills that you want to model.
- Think aloud the ways that you monitor and adjust your thinking to assess your understanding. (See Figure 4.3. You may be modeling not only talk but also actions—i.e., drawing, writing, or moving—that you do to make sense of the learning.)
- As students catch on, ask them to share other ways they may have gotten to the same understanding.

Figure 4.3   Inspiring Image: Think Aloud

What it looks like	What it sounds like
Ms. Alberson stands at the overhead with sample text displayed. Students observe the teacher, and they listen as she works through a difficult piece of text and talks about her thinking. The teacher makes notes about her thinking and about her reading for students to see.	"As I'm reading this text about pruning trees, I notice that it refers to 'hardwoods' and that makes me start to wonder if the tree that I need to prune would fall into this category. I'm going to make a note here in the margin that means I need to find out more information about this."

Explicit Instruction

What It Is

- Explicit teaching involves breaking down a learning task into small parts or steps and teaching each of those steps individually through explanation, demonstration, modeling/thinking aloud, and student practice.

- Explicit teaching provides guided instruction for students in learning new topics or skills. Students then elaborate on their new learning through discourse, practice, writing, etc.

How-To

The steps for explicit teaching are as follows (see Figure 4.4):

- Set a purpose for learning. (Make it relevant!)
- Tell students what to do step by step.
- Show them step by step how to do it.
- Monitor their application of the new learning.

Figure 4.4   Inspiring Image: Explicit Instruction

What it looks like	What it sounds like
Mr. Eton writes on the board "Two Column Notes" and underneath writes, "So What? Why should I learn to do this Mr. E?"	"We are learning to take two column notes today. This strategy is a great way to help you make more sense of anything you read. It can be used for textbook reading, for things you enjoy reading, and maybe even someday in your jobs. You can get a lot of mileage out of this strategy in several different places so it's a great one to be able to do. So, I'm going to show you step by step how to do this. First, make two columns and add a heading that will help you determine . . ."

Scaffolding

What It Is

- When teaching a new concept or strategy, the teacher realizes that students need a great deal of support.
- Through modeling and explicit teaching, the teacher creates a safe environment for learning the new information until the students begin to ask self-regulatory questions about their learning.
- As the teacher sees that students are "getting it," the teacher gradually removes the support to allow students to try their independence (gradual release of responsibility; Pearson, 1983).
- Some students may still be unable to achieve independence, so the teacher brings back the support system to help those students experience success until they are able to achieve independence. (For more information on scaffolding, see Collins, Brown, & Newman, 1986; Vygotsky, 1978.)

How-To

- Present the new strategy.
- Model the skill.
- Think aloud while you or the students make decisions.
  - *Example*: "Today we are going to be talking about 'reflecting.' This skill is absolutely essential for anything you do—whether it's schoolwork, a craft or project, or even working with other

people. When you reflect, you look back at your work and decide what was working and what you would change if you did it again. I'm going to show you how I would reflect on my own work. Let's look at this paper that I wrote a long time ago when I was in college."

- Monitor and adjust difficulty during guided practice.
- Start with less complex information and gradually increase the complexity.
- Complete part of the task for the students.
- Present the material in small steps.
    o *Example*: "Here are three things I want you to reflect on today: What were you successful or good at, examples that show your successes or what you felt good about, and what was new or surprising to you?"
- Provide a variety of ways for students to practice.
- Provide teacher-led practice.
- Engage students in reciprocal teaching.
- Have students work in small groups.
    o *Example*: "You are going to be working in a small group today to reflect on yesterday's homework. I'd like you to talk to your partner about how you feel you are doing. Your partner's job is to ask you questions to help you reflect deeper. Partners, you need to come up with the questions you want your partner to reflect on."
- Offer regular feedback.
- Provide teacher and student feedback.
- Design checklists for self-reflection.
- Share models of expert work.
    o *Example*: "I really like the questions that Susie was asking; I noticed that some people were not really giving specific examples in their reflections—some were being pretty general. As a partner, be aware of that and try to ask them to give an example to help your partner go deeper."
- Increase student responsibility (as students show they can do it).
- Begin to diminish prompts and models.
- Gradually increase complexity and difficulty of information.
- Gradually decrease student support.
    o *Example*: "Okay, we've been practicing being more self-reflective. I'm handing back yesterday's work, and I'd like you to write reflections about the work you've done on this 3 x 5 card. You might want to consider looking at quality or how your thinking has changed."
- Provide independent practice.
- Provide extensive practice opportunities.
- Help students to apply and transfer the learning to new situations.
    o *Example*: "Okay, we've been practicing being more self-reflective. Tonight for homework I would like you to do a quick write. I would like you to reflect on this question, 'How has reflecting helped you to become a better learner?' Yes, I get it. You are reflecting on reflecting!"

Modeling, explicitly teaching, and scaffolding the five vital know-hows will help students to take ownership of their learning. Of course, students cannot master all of these skills immediately. Just like learning to hit a baseball or play an expert game of chess, mastering lifelong learning tools requires continual coaching and practice. This means that teachers in all grade levels and all subject areas need to teach the vital know-hows. The best teaching is a balance between explicitly teaching vital skills, encouraging students to own new learning, and seeing that students can reflect on their growth. The apprenticeship model of teaching sends students out of our classrooms with the skills they need to become lifelong learners.

ELEMENTARY EXAMPLES OF HOW TO TEACH THE VITAL KNOW-HOWS

The rest of this chapter offers simple strategies for teaching the vital know-hows to elementary students. Remember that to really have students own these strategies you need to model, think aloud, explicitly teach and scaffold instruction, and then *expect* your students to own these skills. When you teach using this apprenticeship approach, students will leave your classroom with a learning toolkit they can use year after year.

Reflect/Pair/Share: Reflective Thinking

The Benefits

- Students deepen their thinking about how they learn through collaborative talk with others.
- Students are given an emotionally supportive environment for reevaluating ideas and conclusions.
- Students are prompted to support ideas with reasons and evidence.

How-To

- The teacher develops question prompts that guide students toward self-reflective thinking. (See Resources for a Reflect/Pair/Shareguide and prompts.)
- Students are given wait time to reflect independently on the prompts. (Depending on their age, students can also write down their thoughts—Reflect/Write/Pair/Share.)
- Once students have time to formulate their thoughts, they turn and talk with a buddy, sharing their reflections with each other.
- The teacher then calls on students for a whole class share.
  - Teachers have students' names on popsicle sticks or index cards so they can call on students randomly.

Example

> "Okay, class, I want you to reflect on and think about the following question, quietly, in your heads, not out loud just yet. What do you do when you get stuck as a reader?"
>
> The teacher gives the students time to think.
>
> "Okay, now turn to your talk partner, knee-to-knee, eye-to-eye. Partner A, please share your reflection first. When you hear the chimes, is it Partner B's turn to share."
>
> Each student is given the same amount of time to share. Teacher floats about the room listening to students talk.
>
> "Now, I am going to have Noel draw names from our popsicle sticks. When your name is called, please share your reflection about what you do as a reader. When I call on you, you can't say, 'I don't know.' You must say something. You can ask your partner for help."
>
> The teacher has several students share their ideas. The teacher may choose to record the ideas on the board or on paper, so that students can see the varying thoughts and ideas.
>
> Students turn back to their partners and share what strategies they are already using and which ones they are going to try out.

Levels of Talk: Discourse

The Benefits

- Students learn to deepen their thinking through deepening their level of talk.
- Students who can talk deeply are more likely to read with greater comprehension and write with greater clarity.

How-To

- The first level of talk is to make **Any Comment.** Students are encouraged to say aloud any experience, any thought, any comment, about the topic that is open for discussion. This level of talk allows every student to be able to contribute to the conversation.
- Next students are encouraged to make a **Connecting Comment.** At this level, they need to say something meaningful about the book, topic, or information and connect it to the ongoing conversation. Connecting comments can be made about information learned or in response to people. When connecting to other people's comments, students are taught to do the following:
  - **Say something back.** Students are taught to respond to what others have said. They can add on, agree or disagree with what's

already been said. Some sentence tags that help students stretch the conversation are as follows:

+ I agree because . . .
+ I disagree because . . .
+ I'd like to piggyback on that . . .
+ I'd like to add . . .
+ Another way . . .
+ That reminds me of . . .
+ That connects to . . .
+ I'd like to ask a question about . . .

• Students begin to deepen their talk even further when they learn to make a **Deeper Comment.** Now they need to find words and explain what they mean when others are confused. They are encouraged to stretch out their ideas, explain their thinking, and tell what they mean by using more words.

   o clarify—explain thinking
   o extend—lengthen ideas
   o process—explain how thinking has changed
   o stimulate—ask for ideas, invite discussion, ask for perspectives

Example

This example has the teacher giving prompts to stimulate the depth of the conversation. As students get more adept at this talk, the teacher should begin to remove herself from the conversation as much as possible and let the students lead.

Teacher: Okay, class, let's practice and deepen our talking skills today as we discuss the latest chapters of our Read Aloud book. Can someone get us started with *any comment* about what we've been reading about in the beginning of *Star Girl*?

Betsy: A new girl has come to the school and everybody wonders who she is. (Say anything.)

Teacher: Would anybody like to add to this? (Prompt for connected comment.)

Calvin: Yeah, I'd like to add to that. She's weird and everybody's curious about her. So am I! Playing the ukulele at lunch? Too weird! (Connected comment.)

Teacher: What do you think might be going on with her? (Prompt for deeper comment.)

Juanita: I think she might be crazy, like, mental. Like, maybe she escaped from somewhere and showed up at the school. (Deeper comment; clarify.)

Charles: I disagree. I think she just comes from a different background. She was home schooled and maybe she just doesn't know how to act like other kids do. I have a friend who is home-schooled and he's kinda different. (Connected and deeper comment; extending.)

(Continued)

(Continued)

Teacher: Is anybody wondering about what happened in the opening chapter? (Prompt for deeper comment.)

Noel: Yeah! Why would the author include that opening chapter about the guy getting the mystery porcupine tie in the mail if it wasn't somehow connected to this Star Girl Character? There's a mystery going on here. What do you guys think? (Deeper comment; stimulating.)

The teacher notes the levels of talk and discusses them with the students so the students can note how to connect and deepen their talk, which in turn deepens their thinking!

Anticipation Guides: Reading for Understanding

The Benefits

- Students are better able to access prior knowledge.
- Students develop predicting skills.
- Comprehension and retention of information is increased.
- Reading is more *fun*!

How-To

- Teacher selects important concepts that are to be stressed (see Figure 4.5).
- Teacher develops agree/disagree statements to match the chosen concepts.
- Students read statements and make predictions.
- Students read the material.
- After reading, students review their predictions and discuss.

Example

Figure 4.5   Examples of Anticipation Guides

Kindergarten

Teacher says the following prompts aloud and records the number of "agree" and "disagree" responses.

1. ____ Butterflies use their antennae to smell.

2. ____ Baby butterflies look like big butterflies, only smaller.

3. ____ Butterflies eat worms.

4. ____ Butterflies can only fly when it's warm.

***Star Girl* Anticipation Guide – Fifth Grade**

Directions: Before we read this story, please put a check next to those statements that you agree with in the **BEFORE** column. Compare your opinions with a partner's opinions and discuss your reasons for checking or not checking each statement. After we have read this book, please go back and check those statements you now agree with under the **AFTER** column.

BEFORE   AFTER

_____   _____   It's important to be popular even if it means you have to change how you are.

_____   _____   People who act differently are just weird and should be left alone.

_____   _____   It's important to have lots of friends rather than one or two friends.

_____   _____   When people believe in themselves, they can stand up for their beliefs.

_____   _____   We can learn many lessons from people who are not like us.

Note-Taking: Writing for Understanding

The Benefits

- Students develop a method for effective information gathering.
- Students learn that writing is a valuable skill for processing learning.

How-To

- Teacher selects a note-taking framework appropriate for the age and ability of the students (see Figure 4.6).
- The teacher models and scaffolds instruction in
  - determining important from interesting information
  - summarizing key ideas
  - using abbreviations and symbols
- Students now begin to take their own notes.
- Teacher and students assess growth in note-taking skills.

Example

Figure 4.6   Examples of Note-Taking Strategies

Regions of the U.S.: Data Table Third Grade	
Describe the geography of your region (Examples: landforms, plants, etc.)	• _____
Describe the economy of your region (Examples: natural resources, work, etc.)	• _____
List the cultural characteristics of your region (Examples: ethnicity, work, etc.)	• _____

(Continued)

(Continued)

Draw or List 3 Bugs	In kindergarten, the teacher models data gathering and note-taking on chart paper with the whole class. As she is modeling, she talks about the importance of writing and drawing to keep track and help students remember what they learned.
• buderfles • bez • fles	As students catch on, the teacher can begin to give the students very simple forms and have them begin to collect their own data.

KWHL: Inquiry

The Benefits

- Students connect to their prior knowledge to guide.
- Students are encouraged to ask questions.
- Students learn ways for seeking answers.

How-To

- Students either choose or are given a topic to study.
- Students generate a list of what they think they **know** about the topic already (see Figure 4.7).
- Students then generate a second list of questions about what they **wonder** or want to know about this topic.
- Students then brainstorm and plan **how** and where they will search to find the answers to their questions.
- Finally students plan a way to share what they have **learned** about their topic.

Example

Figure 4.7   Example of KWHL

Know	Wonder	How	Learned
Butterflies have wings.	What do they eat?	A book on butterflies.	Butterflies eat liquids like water or nectar.

Jigsaw: Collaboration

The Benefits

- Students experience the power of collaboration with people of all backgrounds.

- Students learn to become "experts" in an area of study.
- Students develop skills for teaching others.
- Students discover the value of collaborating and relying on others.

How-To

- Students are divided into groups of three–five. The groups should be diverse in terms of gender, ethnicity, race, and ability.
- Teacher appoints one student from each group as the leader. Initially, this person should be the most mature student in the group.
- Teacher divides the day's lesson into five–six segments. For example, if you want history students to learn about Martin Luther King Jr., you might divide a short biography of his life into segments on (1) his childhood, (2) his family life, (3) his beliefs, (4) his activism, and (5) his death and legacy.
- Teacher assigns each student to study and become an expert on a section of King's life, making sure students only have content about their section.
- Teacher allows students time to read over their section at least twice and become familiar with it, perhaps taking notes. (Model how to do this first.)
- Students form temporary "expert groups" by having one student from each jigsaw group join other students assigned to the same segment. Teacher should give students in these expert groups time to discuss the main points of their segment and to rehearse the presentations they will make to their jigsaw group.
- Students return to their original jigsaw groups.
- Each student presents his or her segment to the group. Teacher encourages others in the group to ask questions for clarification and/or take notes with a guided note-taking frame.
- Teacher floats from group to group, observing the process and helping students troubleshoot as needed. Eventually, it's best for the group leader to handle this task. Leaders can be trained by whispering an instruction on how to intervene, until the leader gets the hang of it.
- At the end of the session, teacher determines how to assess the material (with a quiz or project) so that students realize that they are accountable for what they learned.

Kindergarten Example

Teacher says, "At each table there are pictures of insects. I am going to give each group a body part of an insect to investigate. Once you have had time to study your special area, you will be meeting with another group to share what each of you has learned about insects."

In a group of three, each student studies his own part of an insect. Students then number off One, Two, and Three in their group. The Ones get together

(Continued)

(Continued)

and count insect legs. The Twos study body sections. The Threes look for antennae. In their body part groups, they agree on what they learned and what they will share with the other groups. They then go back to their original group and share what they each learned (six legs, three body sections, two antennae).

Next time, they can look at several bugs and determine whether they are insects or not based on the legs and body parts.

The following strategies can be exceptionally powerful because, depending on how you use them, they combine two or more of the vital-know hows.

Learning Logs

The Benefits

- Students are taught and encouraged to apply reflective thinking, writing for understanding, collaboration, discourse, and inquiry.
- Students are provided with a safe rehearsal place.
- Teachers can better encourage total participation.
- Students are provided with a place to make sense of new information.
- Students are prompted to
  o observe
  o think about their own thinking
  o make connections between content and life
- Students' retention of new learning is increased.
- Students are provided with a place for formative assessment.
- Teachers are able to get to know their students better.
- Sharing entries from logs helps students be prepared for classroom discussions.

How-To

- Each student has a composition book for noting personal reflections.
- At times, the teacher provides prompts; other times, students decide what they want to write about.
- Students write in logs a few times a week, when it is a natural and appropriate time to reflect or process.
- Teacher collects the logs once or twice a marking period, reads and comments on a few entries that students want them to read.
- Students receive points for increased fluency. Teachers should not grade or mark for spelling, punctuation, correctness of ideas, etc. Logs are meant to be a *safe* place for rehearsing ideas.
- Logs can be used as a place to inquire.
- Students can share and exchange ideas through talking about log entries.

Example

> A student writes, "I am confused about what I am supposed to do with the math today. I get how to make decimals into fractions, but reducing is always hard for me. I asked Betsy for help. She said I need to find a number that will divide into both the top and the bottom number. If the numbers are even, I can divide by 2 for sure."
>
> "I guess I just need to keep practicing and it will get easier."

Interactive Vocabulary

The Benefits

- Students are encouraged to use reflective thinking, reading and writing for understanding, collaboration, discourse, and inquiry.
- Students are provided guidance and modeling with learning new words.
- Students learn new words through varying learning modalities.
- Students process in nonlinguistic ways that provide for deeper understanding.
- Students embrace the key idea that they can help one another clear up misconceptions through discourse.

How-To

(We call this process "Dr. Dr. Toilet Paper" to help us and students remember the steps.) The teacher prompts the students with the following (see Figure 4.8):

- **Describe**, explain, or give an example of a new term. (For example, use visual images, video or picture images, stories that use the term, etc.)
- **Restate** the description, explanation, or example *in their own words.*
- **Draw** a picture, symbol, or graphic representation of the term or phrase.
- **Review** and deepen understanding of the term, adding new information and going deeper.
- **Talk** and discuss terms with one another in think-pair-share partnerships.
- **Play** and/or create games that allow students to cement the new terms. (Example: matching/concentration games, vocabulary charades, etc.)

Example

> **Figure 4.8** Example of Interactive Vocabulary
>
> Molecules
>
> - The teacher says, "People have personalities, and so do things. Rubber bands are stretchy and soap is slippery. A thing's personality comes from the way its molecules on the inside behave. Molecules are the super-super-tiny bits that make up all things. The way rubber molecules link up to each other makes it stretchy. The way soap molecules hold onto each other makes soap slippery."
> - Students restate their own words, "Molecules are really little and make up things."
> - Students draw their own images of a molecule.
> - Review: "Molecules are very small. You can't see them with your eyes."
> - Talk: Students talk to each other, look at their pictures, and share what they know about molecules. Teacher floats around the room and listens to talk.
> - Practice: Play a matching game with their science words.

See Resources for early and upper elementary Interactive Vocabulary Log Templates.

Graphic Organizers

Teachers today know that graphic organizers are powerful learning tools to use in classroom instruction. (In this book, we define graphic organizers as any visual diagrams such as cluster maps, webbing, KWL charts, Venn diagrams, brainstorming charts, etc.)

The Benefits

- Students are taught and encouraged to apply reflective thinking, reading and writing for understanding, collaboration, discourse, and inquiry.
- Students' thinking is activated.
- Students retrieve prior knowledge with increased proficiency.
- Students link new information with the old. (This is how the brain learns best!)
- Students retain and transfer knowledge.
- Students can visualize the learning process.

How-To

- Graphic organizers should be made *big* and *alive*, using chart paper and markers. Students work in groups of three to brainstorm ideas, then post their graphic organizers around the room for other students to see. Groups can then walk around the room and look at other groups' graphic organizers. With a clipboard and appointed recorder, they can write any information that they didn't include on their map. Then, when they return back to their own maps, they can add the information they learned from their peers.

- Organizers shouldn't be run as dittos! Instead, a model of a graphic organizer can be made and modeled on the overhead to show how this structure helps organize thinking. Students can then create their own visual maps as long as these meet the criteria you are asking for in the lesson. Students who want to use your sample framework may do so. You can also have some copies of your map for students who really struggle with developing their own schema.

- In the early elementary grades, model using graphic organizers with the whole class, showing and thinking aloud how to plan and process organizing your thoughts. When you feel like students are ready, give them some blank paper and let them have a go at creating their own simple organizer. Introduce one type of organizer at a time, then let students choose which way they want to organize their ideas. Encourage students who are making their own choices; this will lead others to try choosing for themselves.

- Graphic organizers can chart and show growth in the learning process. At the end of a marking period, put up chart paper with a circle in the middle that states, "What we learned in (subject area) this marking period." As students share things they have learned, write the information on the chart and put each student's initials under his or her comment. (Students love seeing their names on the charts.) Create a new map each marking period. Take previous quarters' maps out, and add the new ones so students can see how much they have grown as learners. This is especially powerful for struggling learners because they don't visualize themselves as learners.

- Some students struggle with finding main ideas or categories to use when organizing information in their cluster maps. Give those students what they need to succeed by giving them a list of the categories of information to include on their map. Challenge the more advanced students to find their own categories.

- Students love creating graphic organizers on computers. This adds novelty, and the learning brain loves novelty. Some quality computer programs for graphic organizers are Inspiration and Kidspiration (and these programs are easy to use).

- Mapping is an excellent strategy for learning vocabulary. Vocabulary maps allow students to explore a word in various ways. Students can create their own vocabulary maps, or they can work with a partner or small group to create maps. Have students keep a vocabulary journal in a spiral notebook or composition book. This will give students a log of their vocabulary learning and will also keep you away from the copy machine.
  - Groups can create a map for different words and then teach each other their words using their maps. Keep the maps posted in the room so that students can keep learning from them.
  - Teachers can assign one or two "Must Do" categories and then allow students to choose two categories of their own.

o Some categories for vocabulary mapping may include the following (teachers should select several categories that are appropriate for the age and subject level they are teaching):

+ guessing the meaning (prefixes, suffixes, root words)
+ what is it/describing the word
+ antonyms/opposite words
+ synonyms/related words
+ analogies/similes/metaphors ("This is like . . . ")
+ examples from text (number problems, experiments, etc.)
+ examples from life
+ TV/movie examples
+ using word in sentence
+ connecting to related concepts
+ pictures/drawing

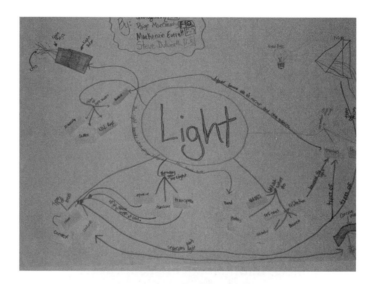

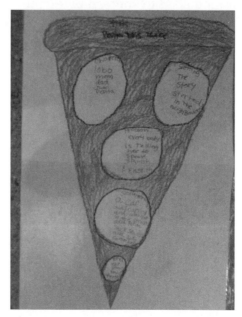

SOURCE: Photos courtesy of Lisa Rando (Frost Elementary School, Jackson, MI).

TIPS FOR TEACHING VITAL KNOW-HOW STRATEGIES

1. Always begin by telling students they will be learning a strategy. Explain how the strategy will empower them as learners not only in school but also in life.

2. The first time you teach a new strategy, think aloud and model how to use the strategy to the whole class.

3. After modeling the strategy to the whole class, begin scaffolding instruction by asking the students who are first catching on to share their thinking. Watch as more and more students catch on before letting them have a go at it on their own.

4. If you still have a few students who are struggling, you can work with them or have another student pair up and work with that student.

When we, at each grade level, in age-appropriate ways, teach students the vital know-hows, they will begin to internalize and transfer these skills into their daily learning lives.

In the next three chapters, we will look at "Lite-n-Lean Strategies," "Deep-n-Dynamic Lesson Designs," and "Assessment Tools" that allow students to practice independence and ownership of their own learning. (For a list of more resources for teaching the vital know-hows, see Resources.)

INSPIRING SNAPSHOT

Student With Special Needs Is Empowered With Vital Know-Hows

Brad, a student with a learning disability, had a very difficult year as a third grader. He had chronic attendance problems, behavior issues, and poor grades. In fourth grade, he came to me for two hours a day for resource room language arts and study skills. In both classes I explicitly taught my students the vital know-hows and how to be self-reflective learners. I modeled not only learning strategies, but strategies for getting organized, building self-esteem, and self-monitoring. Brad started to really "get it," and began applying his new skills in the classroom. Becoming a self-reflective learner made such a difference in Brad's view of himself and his abilities that in fifth grade he made the honor roll all year! By middle school, he was on consultation and not in special education classes! I asked Brad if he would come in and talk to my fifth grade students about what he had learned about himself.

Here's what he said: "When I was in third grade, I didn't know how to learn very well and I felt like a dummy. Then in fourth grade I started to learn these strategies and I realized I could learn. Now when I walk down the hall people say, 'There goes Brad, that smart guy!' Now I do better in my classes and I have a lot more friends!"

5

Flexible Grouping

The only good kind of instruction is that which marches ahead of development and leads it.

—Lev Vygotsky (1978, p. 24)

In an Inspiring Classroom, students can be moved in and out of groups for specific purposes. Flexible grouping allows us to instruct children on the basis of learning needs and interests. When students are grouped according to learning needs, we are better able to teach them at the level they are ready to learn. When children are grouped according to interests, the opportunities to learn from each other are maximized. Flexible groups vary in size, duration of grouping, and can work beyond the classroom (cross-curricular, grade-level teams, etc.).

Effective flexible grouping starts with the teacher preassessing for readiness or interests. (See Chapter 14 for ways to preassess.) Students can then be placed in groups based on what they need to learn or by what they are interested in learning. Why make everyone sit through lessons on skills they already have? For example, if we preassess students for punctuation skills in writing, we can create groups that need to practice using end punctuation, while others who already have that skill can be working on commas. A more advanced group might be working on quotation marks.

Generally, the teacher may begin class with a whole group mini-lesson before breaking students up for small, flexible group instruction. In the mini-lesson, the teacher presents the key ideas for the lesson. The teacher may end the whole group session with a preassessment that helps her create the flexible groups, or she may have all students complete an activity and then begin the flexible groups the following day.

The following charts (Figure 5.1) show the varying ways we might flexibly group in reading, writing, and math, along with examples of what the students are doing in those groups.

Figure 5.1   Examples of Grouping Strategies

Flexible Grouping in Reading		
Group by	*This Means*	*Examples*
Readiness • Skill or Strategy Instruction	The teacher works with students in small groups based on the reading skills or strategies they need to learn.	The teacher preassesses students for reading skills (decoding/comprehension) that are expected for students at that grade level. Students are then grouped to work on the skills they need.
• Content	The teacher works with small groups on reading content that is at their appropriate readiness level.	The teacher selects stories from leveled books, then groups the students based on their reading levels. All groups are reading different texts, but are studying the same element of reading in their books (for example, theme).
Interests • Book Club	Students read and discuss a book of their choice.	The teacher provides choices of books, students rank order their choices and are placed in book club groups based on one of their top choices.
• Genre Studies	Students get together and study a fiction genre.	The teacher provides choices of genres, students rank order their choices and are placed in book club groups based on one of their top choices.
• Nonfiction Choice	Students come together and study a nonfiction topic of their choice.	The teacher provides choices of nonfiction topics, students rank order their choices and are placed in book club groups based on one of their top choices.

Flexible Groups in Writing		
Group by	*This Means*	*Examples and Information*
Readiness • Skill or Strategy Instruction	The teacher works with students in small groups based on the writing skills or strategies they need to learn.	The teacher preassesses students for writing skills (grammar, punctuation) and then works with the groups based on the writing skills they need to develop.
Interests • Genre Studies	Students get together to study how to write a certain genre.	The teacher provides models of genres (mystery, folk tales, memoirs) and works with groups to hone their skills in writing that genre.
• Strategy/Style Studies	Students choose a writing skill or technique.	Students select a writing skill or technique they want to practice in their writing (voice, leads, or description) and they work with each other and the teacher to build those skills or techniques.

(Continued)

(Continued)

Flexible Groups in Math		
Group by	*This Means*	*Examples and Information*
Readiness • Skill or Strategy Instruction	The teacher works with students in small groups based on the math skills they need to learn.	The teacher preassesses students for math skills (computation, problem solving, recall) and then works with groups based on the math skills they need to develop.
• Depth of Content	The teacher works with small groups on appropriate depth of math content for that group.	Students who are struggling with the math concept being taught may work on simpler practice problems with additional support materials such as manipulatives or calculators. Students who already grasp the concept can work on real life applications or logic-problem solving applications.
Interests	Students choose a math skill they want to develop.	Students choose a geometric shape of interest and become group experts on it, teaching others what they have learned.

MANAGING FLEXIBLE GROUPS

While we are working with a small group, the other students need to be taught and expected to work independently on other assignments. We need to plan how we want to set up independent work time and then specifically teach, model, and scaffold instruction about what students are expected to do during that time. The following management suggestions help create a classroom that thrives with independent, responsible learners.

Independent Work Time

- Give students classroom assignments.
  - o Problems or questions from textbook.
  - o Work on a long-term project or task such as a research paper, independent reading book, or math project.
- Have students work in learning centers you have set up in the room. Centers can be set up in varying ways (see Figure 5.2).
  - o Students can be assigned to a specific center.
  - o Teacher labels names of centers and who is assigned to which center where students can see them.
  - o Students can sign up for the center where they want to work.
  - o Only a certain number of students are allowed at each center at one time, so if a center is full, they must choose another.

Figure 5.2   Centers by Subject Area

Possible Types of Centers by Subject Area		
Reading Centers	*Writing Centers*	*Math Centers*
Partner Reading	Peer Editing Center	Skill Practice Center
Fluency Center	Peer Revision Center	Problem Solving Center
Strategy Center	Style Practice Center	Real Life Math Center
Internet Research	Writing Research Center	Internet or Calculator Math
Content Area Project	Content Area Writing Center	Hands-On Math Center
Independent Reading	Mentor Text Center	Math Literacy Center

- Use learning contracts as illustrated in Figure 5.3.
  - Students are given work contracts that they must complete over a set time period.

Figure 5.3   Sample Contracts

Sample Reading Contract

Name: _____

This week during my independent reading time, I agree to work on and complete the following:

_____ Read _____ pages of my independent reading book

_____ Write _____ entries in my reading log

_____ Complete the vocabulary skills sheets/activities

_____ Reread my guided reading book with a partner

_____ Write a summary of what my guided reading book is about

Sample Math Contract

Name: _____

Today during my math time, I agree to:

_____ Work on my practice problems

_____ Work with a learning buddy to review today's assignment

_____ Use the cubes to help me, then put the cubes all back where they belong

- Have students work on anchor activities.
  - Anchor activities, which are important in the daily classroom structure and routine, are essential in flexible grouping. (See Resources for a list of ideas for anchor activities.)

o Students move independently, to self-directed projects, assignments, activities that are ongoing (journaling, reflecting, self-assessing, etc.), a review of skills, or a deeper treatment of current learning targets.

Asking for Help

When you are working with a group, the other students need to be taught what to do if they need help.

- Have students first try to figure things out on their own, or try to get help from their other group members. (Teach students that they must try to get help from three other students before coming to you for help. This is called the "See three before me" policy.)
- If students exhaust the other options and still need help, develop a procedure for letting you know they need help from you. Some possible procedures might be the following:
  o The student writes his name on the board. The teacher checks the board frequently while working with other groups and calls the student over for help.
  o The teacher finds a stop point in her group work and asks if anyone needs help.
  o Students have a stack of cups at their desk or table. A red cup at the top means the student is stuck and needs help. A yellow cup means they could use help or talk with a classmate. A green cup means they are working just fine on their own.

Getting Materials

Students need to be taught how to get and return materials, so they do not disrupt you while they are working. Here are some suggestions for getting and returning materials.

- Have a sign out/sign in sheet for students to get and return materials on their own.
- Assign specific students to be responsible for passing out and collecting materials.
- If you are using centers, have the necessary materials ready in an organized box at each center. Have students put everything back in the box when they are finished in the center.

Assessing Independent Work

It's important to gather data and assess the independent work that students are doing in ways that are practical and doable for you and the students. Some suggestions for assessing independent work are below.

- Collect specific assignments and grade them or have students grade them in groups.
- Have students keep a portfolio of their daily or weekly work. When it's time to assess, have students select something that they want you to assess and then you select one other item to assess.

- Have students assess with peers.
  - Students find a partner to talk over new learning.
  - While students are talking, you float about the room gathering anecdotal evidence of their learning.
- Have students self-assess.
  - Create mini-checklists of learning goals or tasks and have them assess their progress and understandings; for example, "What was confusing for me? What did I do well? What deserves more of my energy and focus next time?"

Flexible grouping not only allows us to teach more effectively what students need to learn, but when teachers teach students to manage themselves and work responsibly, they give them tools they need to become independent, lifelong learners.

INSPIRING SNAPSHOT

Flexible Grouping Makes My Life Better, Too!

I had an aha! moment when I gave myself permission to group students flexibly. I knew that there were times when my students needed to learn at different levels of depth and complexity, but since I had lived in a one-size-fits-all world of teaching, I didn't think I could do that.

What I discovered when I started using flexible groups, first in reading and then in math, was that all my students felt more successful because they were learning within their zone of proximal development. (I call it the Goldilocks' Theory—the learning can't be too easy and it can't be too hard; it needs to be *just right*!) When I preassessed my students and grouped them so that I could work directly with groups at their readiness level, not only did they do better, but I was less crazy. I was not running around the room like a mad woman trying to help the struggling learners scattered around the room, or trying to challenge the advanced learners who were finished and bored. Each group was getting what they needed. They were all happier and stayed more engaged.

Another added benefit I discovered when grouping flexibly is my students learned to be more independent. For the most part, they took this "new" responsibility seriously and I realized that they could do *way* more on their own than I thought they could!

6

Teaching
for Meaning

Enduring understandings provide a larger purpose for learning targeted content. They implicitly answer the question, "Why is this worth knowing?"

—Jay McTighe

The brain understands best when it sees the learning as relevant. In this chapter, you will learn to design your lessons using our C U KAN framework to assure that your lessons are engaging and connected to the lives of your students, and also to help students attain curriculum objectives.

WHAT IS C U KAN?

We like to pronounce it "See you can!" to help us remember the important components of meaningful lessons. C U KAN is an acronym for those components (see Figure 6.1). When planning a unit or lesson, this framework will help us clarify the objectives, or learning target, for the lesson. Our framework is adapted from the work of Jay McTighe and Carol Ann Tomlinson (2006).

WHY C U KAN?

Designing engaging and meaningful lessons becomes effective and efficient when we use the C U KAN framework. The C U KAN framework lets us begin with the end in mind and helps us do the following:

1. C U KAN provides a target for meaningful learning.

    For Us: If we want students to be engaged in our content and lessons, we must design lessons that connect to our students and

Figure 6.1   C U KAN Components

Concept
The **Concept** is the big overarching idea of a unit or lesson. The concept is *not* the topic of the lesson, such as "consonant blends" or "subtraction." It is very global, broad, and can be applied across subject areas. The concept is usually one word such as "change" or "relationships."
At the elementary grades, teaching to a concept will allow you to design thematic units.
Understand
The **Understandings** are the underlying principles embedded within the concepts. Understandings answer the question, "Why is it important to know this?" and help us connect the content to students' lives. When developing understandings for our lessons, adding the word "that" (*Understand that . . .*) helps us move away from teaching just facts and knowledge toward teaching the big ideas that are the heart of our subject, such as "Understand that change happens over time."
Know
The **Know** includes the key facts and key vocabulary that enables students to speak to the understandings. They are often examples of the Understandings, or facts, related to the understanding. The facts are content specific such as, "Michigan is surrounded by the Great Lakes" or "The main characters in *Charlotte's Web* are Charlotte and Wilbur."
Able To Do
The **Able To Do** skills are the social skills, production skills, fundamental skills, or skills of the discipline that students need to be able to do as they work toward the understandings. **Able To Do** objectives might be "able to work in groups," "able to read a chart," or "able to create a graphic organizer."
Now You Get It!
The **Now You Get It** is the way that students demonstrate understanding (transfer) of the targeted learning objectives. The **Now You Get It!** can occur during and after learning by using exit cards, tests and quizzes, and various performance-based assessments.

their world. The C U KAN framework points out global applications, underlying principles, and key important information that helps us make learning relevant for students.

For Our Students: Our students want to know and deserve to know how the content we teach connects to their world. Using the C U KAN framework allows us to give a meaningful response to the question, "Why do we have to know this?" We will be able to respond to students by explaining such things as, "Good readers have a toolbox of strategies that help them make sense of text. Today, we are going to add another important tool to your toolbox, so that you can grow your good reader skills." With meaningful learning targets, students will know how the learning connects to their lives.

2. C U KAN provides a target for meaningful instruction.

For Us: Being clear about the learning target before we write our daily lessons ensures that the activities we design to Chunk, Chew, and Check our lessons are really hitting our target and are not simply busy work. A clear learning target helps us to plan instructional options that reach all our students. For example, we can plan for students who need information visually, students who learn best through discussions, or students who need language support. The C U KAN framework also frees us from teaching to the book. It helps us discern what parts of the book support the learning target and where other resources would better hit the target. For example, we don't need to teach ten vocabulary terms just because our textbook has bolded ten vocabulary terms in Chapter 3. A clear learning target allows us to make better choices about which words our students most need to know in order to deeply understand, apply, and transfer the learning.

For Our Students: When the learning target is clear, our students can shift their thinking from "What am I supposed to be learning?" to "What is the best way for me to learn this?" How can students possibly select a learning strategy to help them hit the target when they don't know what the target is? A clear learning target allows students to use their time more efficiently by studying in a way that works for them.

3. C U KAN provides a target for meaningful assessment.

For Us: Our assessment options become clear when we ask, "How can students best demonstrate that they understand the learning target?" When we know our target and we know our students, we can better determine whether to offer choices, tier our lessons, or let students do independent learning contracts. We can also save ourselves valuable class time by preassessing to determine what our students already know or don't know about the learning target. This information helps us to prioritize our time and focus on what students really need to learn.

For Our Students: Clear learning targets help our students reflect on and assess their own learning growth. Posting the learning target where students can clearly see it is a continual reminder to them about where they are going. When students know where they are going, they can assess what they have mastered and what they have yet to learn.

HOW TO WRITE A C U KAN

Figure 6.2 shows a sample of the Concept, Understanding, Knowledge, Able To Do (Skills), and Now You Get It for several different content areas.

Figure 6.2 CU KAN Sample Learning Targets

	Social Studies	Science	Math	Language Arts
Concept *The big idea of a unit/lesson, usually one word*	Community (second grade)	Force (fifth grade)	System (first grade)	System (kindergarten)
Understand *The underlying principle that connects the content to students' lives.*	Understand that in a community there is an interaction between the people and the natural environment	Understand that humans study how nature works and use that knowledge to create things that make life easier for humans	Understand that people made up the idea of time as a way to measure how long events or actions take place and so they can organize and plan	Understand that humans created a system of sounds and symbols so that they could communicate effectively
Know *The key facts and key vocabulary words that support the understandings.*	The natural and human characteristics of where we live	Six types of simple machines Force, distance, work	Hour Half Hour Half Past the Hour	Each letter of the alphabet produces its own sound The sound of each letter is the code that allows humans to communicate
Able To Do *The basic skills, social skills, production skills, and/or skills of the discipline students will be able to do to work toward the understandings.*	Use graphic aides like maps or pictures Gather data about our community	Create a Compare/Contrast chart that shows the different types of simple machines Calculate the amount of work $(F \times D = W)$	Tell time to the hour and half hour	Identify the letters of the alphabet and their sounds
Now You Get It! *The way students demonstrate their understanding of the above learning objectives.*	RAFT Plus Role play a person from the community and tell how you interact with the environment	Centers Students rotate through six centers, one on each machine The complete activities and the compare/contrast chart	Tiered Lesson Tier 1: Students work on telling time with a digital or analog clock Tier 2: Students create a daily schedule for a typical school day	Choice Students choose one activity/ center from a choice menu that is on the board for students to see

C U KAN SAMPLE

The following is an example of a three- or four-day lesson plan developed using the C U KAN model. C U KAN lessons can be longer projects, like this example, but they can also be short one-day lessons, homework, or even ongoing class work. Students can also work in groups or independently. Each component was written based on the Learning Target (Figure 6.3), which also appears at the beginning of the student handout (Figures 6.4 and 6.5) for them to have as a reference and reminder of the learning target.

Figure 6.3   Example of a Clear Learning Target

Learning Target
Name: Kathleen Kryza   Grade Level of Lesson: Third

Concept (Overarching Theme): Inspirational Leadership

As a result students should . . .

Understand That (Key principles)

- Dr. Martin Luther King Jr. inspired us to create a world where all people are treated equally.
- You can help to create MLK's dream by creating peace in yourselves and in your community.

Know (Facts)

- Peace, Fairness, Freedom, Equal Rights, Diversity, Nonviolence (You decide which terms you wish students to comprehend)
- Key events in MLK's life

Able To Do (Skills)

- Create a note-taking guide or graphic with important facts about Dr. King.

Now You Get It!

- The assessment will be determined by the structure of the lesson you design.

Rubrics for Student Assessment

Once you have developed the C U KAN framework, you can easily develop the rubric for assessing. Below are steps and suggestions for developing a rubric aligned to your C U KAN outline (see Figure 6.6 on page 60).

- The first two sections of the rubric are simply the Understand and Know of your C U KAN. And guess what? You already developed those at the beginning of your unit. Under the Expectations column of the rubric, add the Understand and Know objectives that you developed.

Figure 6.4   Example of Student Handout and Learning Target

Martin Luther King Jr. Day
Choice Menu

Concept: Inspirational Leadership

Understand:

- Dr. Martin Luther King Jr. inspired us to create a world where all people are treated equally.
- You can help to create MLK's dream by creating peace in yourselves and in your community.

Know:

- Peace, Fair, Freedom, Equal Rights, Diversity, Nonviolence (You decide which terms you wish students to comprehend)
- Key events in Dr. Martin Luther King's life

Able To Do:

- Create a note-taking guide or graphic with important facts about Dr. King.

Now You Get It!:

- Choose one of the activities below to show what you understand and know about MLK's inspirational leadership.

Figure 6.5   Example of Student Handout

Present a skit or video that tells about MLK's vision and what students today can do to help live that vision.	Write a story about the world that MLK imagined.
Make a timeline that tells about MLK's life. Continue the timeline making up events to show when and how you think the world will reach his dream.	Design a peace flag or monument to honor MLK. Write or speak explaining what you created and how this will help carry on the message of MLK's dream.
Write and illustrate a book for younger children about MLK and how they can help create his dream.	Write a rap/poem/song about MLK and his dream.

- The third section of the rubric is Quality Work. Prior to starting work on their projects, students are expected to develop at least three quality criteria specific to their project type (i.e., skit, poster, etc.). The students must be specific and avoid using generic phrases such as, "We'll work hard," "We'll take our time," "It will look good." (See Resources for Ideas for Quality Project Standards.)
- Before the students can work on their projects, review their criteria for Quality Work. Students are not allowed to work on their project until you have initialed the rubric showing your approve of their criteria. This is important because when you are grading the quality section, the students will be graded based on the quality criteria that

Figure 6.6   Example of Rubric

Name(s): _____   _____

Project Choice:

Expectations	Excellent	Good	Okay	Needs Improvement
Shows understanding of MLK's dream and how you can help create the dream ____ points				
Knows facts about MLK's life ____ points				
Quality Work (As defined by you) ____ points				
Notes				
Three Ways I/We Will Do Quality Work for Our Project: 1. _____ 2. _____ 3. _____				
What we/I did that was quality work . . . _____				
What I/we could do better next time . . . _____				
TEACHER COMMENTS				

they committed to achieving on the project. (You said you were going to have costumes and props in your skit, but you don't. That brings your grade down for that section of the rubric.) The younger the students, the fewer and simpler the criteria.

- Any other sections you might want to include on a rubric could be categories such as the following: Work Habits or Group Effort. There could be a section for Notes or Graphic Organizers, or any of the Able To Do skills that you developed under the Able To Do in your C U KAN.

- Depending on the grade level of the students, you can use either words or pictures to note whether students have been successful (excellent) or not so successful (not so good).

- After students have shared their projects, have them self-assess on the rubric by placing check marks in the boxes measuring where they think they performed. (To keep things simple, avoid having them assign themselves points.) They complete the self-assessment by responding to the prompts: "What we did that was Quality

Work . . . " or "What I did that I was proud of" and "What we would do differently next time . . . " Then they turn in the rubric.

- Now, you fill out the same rubric, only you put in the points. You add your grade and comments and return the rubrics to the students.

Using the Rubric With Students

- Students should receive the rubric as they begin to work on their projects. You can give students a copy of the rubric, show it to them on the overhead, or make a wall chart of it. Explain what's expected of them as you walk through the rubric.
- Connect self-assessment in school to the type of reflective self-assessing they will need to do as they enter the work world. Explain to students that they need to do quality work and be able to know when they are doing quality work. As they get better at self-assessing, they should find the scores they give themselves on the rubric become very close to the teacher's scores.
- If you are giving grades, explain to students that the grade you give is the final grade because you are the professional, coach, and guide for their learning. You know what it looks like when they "get it."

C U KAN TEACHING TIPS FOR ALL LESSON DESIGNS

Included below are tips to keep in mind when designing lessons using the C U KAN framework. At the end of Chapters 8–13 on lesson designs, there are teaching tips that are *specific* to that design.

Lesson Design

- Develop the C U KAN for the lesson before you do anything else.
- For your own benefit, it's easier to first write the Understanding in adult language, then simplify it for the grade level of your students.
- The Concept and Understanding usually cover an entire unit while the lessons within that unit will have different Know, Able To Do, and, possibly, Now You Get It.
- All lesson designs can be short-term (Lite-n-Lean) or long-term (Deep-n-Dynamic) assignments. (For example, the lessons could take two days or two weeks, homework or class work.)
- Lessons can be done alone or in groups.

Management

- Develop routines and procedures for things such as how to get materials, move around the room, manage noise level, clean up, work in groups, etc. Practice these procedures until students have them down. If students start to slack off on procedures, kindly have them practice them again.
- Assign students to make sure that the room is tidy and materials are put back where they are supposed to be.

- Students must do quality work on their product choice. Once students have picked their project type and have begun working on it, give them the assessment rubric. Note that Quality Work is one of the expectations on the rubric. At the bottom of the rubric, have students write down criteria that tell *specifically* how they will do quality work for that project type.
  For example, Quality Skit Criteria:
  1. We will use costumes.
  2. We will know our parts.
  3. We will rehearse at least three times.
- Have students develop a plan to show you what they are going to do. If they are working in groups, they must show that they have divided up the tasks so that everyone has a task to do.
- If students will be presenting their projects (skits, songs, etc.) make an advance sign-up sheet for students who need to present. Be very specific regarding how much presentation time will be allowed. (Usually, if students ramble on and use too much time it's because they are not prepared.)
- If you're doing a long-term project, have students become "experts" before they work on the creative part of the project. This is a good time to model and scaffold how to do the vital know-how skills like note-taking or using graphic organizers. Once they show you that they have the content knowledge, they can work on the project.
- While students are working on lessons, be sure to float around the room and check to see that they have the Understand, Know, and Able To Do in their projects.

Assessment

- The rubric should reflect the Understand, Know, Quality Work, and whatever other category you may choose to assess. (See rubric examples in lesson design chapters.)
- Always have students assess themselves on their projects first. Then you assess using the same rubric.
- You can use your C U KAN framework to preassess students prior to beginning a unit. For example, turn your C U KAN objectives into questions and have students write and/or draw what they know about the questions prior to starting the unit. Collect the information and use it to determine what students know and don't know about your topic.
- You can also have students self-assess during the learning process using the C U KAN objectives. For example, in the middle of a lesson or unit, you can ask students to give you a thumbs up if they get the objectives, thumbs sideways if they somewhat get it, and thumbs down if they are still confused. Having students self-reflect on the learning target helps build ownership and responsibility for learning.
- If you are using a rubric to assess, have students assess themselves on the rubric. The goal is for them to be as close to the grade you would give them as possible. (You're the "boss" so your grade counts.)

Teacher Self-Assessment

As you try out new dynamic designs, note what's working and what is not. Keep doing what *is* working, and troubleshoot what's not working.

If you are doing lessons as a group project:

- Assign students in groups by choice, readiness, or learning profile. (If you assign groups by readiness, you can easily tier the assignment.)
- Have the students choose their jobs in the group. (Some jobs could be leader, scribe, teacher-getter, organizer, timekeeper, life coach.) Be sure to have the students be responsible for their jobs.
- As a class, discuss appropriate group behaviors. Design a group behavior rubric based on their discussions.
- Talk about the consequences of not working with the group. (If a person chooses to hurt and not help the group, they can get "fired" from the group and have to work on an independent activity.)
- Have the groups self-assess at the end of each work session. Then you, as their "boss," agree or disagree with their assessment.

HOW C U KAN WILL HELP YOU DIFFERENTIATE

The C U KAN framework helps you differentiate because it gives you a clear map for what you want your students to understand, know, and be able to demonstrate. C U KAN also helps you design an aligned rubric that focuses on the essential learning points. You know what you are looking for and what it looks like when students get there.

C U KAN gives you the road map to begin differentiating:

1. How students take in the C U KAN information (Chunk).

2. How students process the C U KAN information (Chew).

3. How students demonstrate their understanding of the C U KAN (Check).

We can readily convey the importance of content to our students when we have a clear learning target to aim toward and when we make real-life connections to that target. Sharing the learning target encourages students to take responsibility for their own learning. They are able to self-reflect; they know when they are getting or not getting the targeted objectives. Starting with a clear learning target also allows us to think of alternative options for assessing and reporting students' progress toward learning outcomes. See, we *can* reach all types of learners and our learning target, too. Once you have developed your C U KAN framework, designing deep and dynamic lessons and rubrics for assessment is a cinch. So create your C U KAN, try out the following lesson designs, and have fun!

7

Instructional Elements to Differentiate

"How well does the child fit into our program?" "How well is our program fitting the child?"

—Alicia Duncan

Once we have our C U KAN target set, it is time to evaluate the instructional elements we can differentiate to assist our students along the path to learning. In this chapter, we will look more in depth at the five elements you can differentiate demonstrated with sample lessons. Notice in the examples that there are clear outcomes set as the learning goal for each lesson. In some lessons, the outcome is simply the Know portion of the C U KAN. In other lessons the teacher may have Know and Do objectives set as the learning target. Once the outcome is established, the instructional elements are how we begin intentionally responding to our learners' needs. Examining the five instructional elements also helps us to discover parts of the learning process that can help or hinder a particular student from learning the outcomes.

First, let's begin by recalling the five elements (see Figure 7.1) that a teacher can differentiate when designing lessons to meet students' needs:

Chunk: how students take-in or *input* new information

Chew: how students make sense of or *process* the new information

Check: how students show what they know or *output* the new information

The Environment: the tone and the routines of the classroom

The Content: what students learn; depth and complexity or connection to their personal interests

Figure 7.1   Five Elements We Can Differentiate

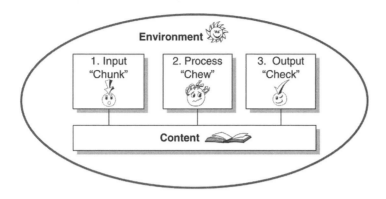

Many of us already differentiate at least one, if not more, of these elements. However, the key to moving forward in our practice is to know *why* we are doing what we are doing. It is not enough to just randomly do activities or apply strategies. Students will be inspired by us when we tell them that our lessons were designed specifically for their unique talents or needs (see Figure 7.2).

Figure 7.2   Inspiring Image: Responding to Learners' Needs

Inspiring Image

"When I was thinking about the best way for our class group to learn today's math lesson, I looked at our learning styles chart on the wall to remind me of the different ways we take in new information. So today, you will have a choice of three different activities for learning about geometric shapes. Once I describe the lessons to you, you can choose the one that best fits your learning style."

CHUNK, CHEW, AND CHECK: GETTING STARTED

Every lesson, every day, begin to think this way:

"Chunk, chew, and check . . . it's how the brain learns best!"

Whether you are reviewing calendar skills, teaching a new unit on heredity, or reminding writers how to incorporate powerful language in their writing, chunk, chew, and check is your key to the most basic differentiation. It is not differentiation when students read a chapter, answer the questions at the end of the chapter, take a test, read a chapter, answer questions, take a test, and so on. These first three elements—chunk, chew, and check—are thought of as "just good teaching" for every single lesson.

ELEMENT 1: CHUNK

*Same learning target, different ways to **input** new information into brains*

Chunk Example 1: Shapes in the Environment

C U KAN Lesson Outcomes

Know: The names of shapes (triangle, triangular prism, square, cube, rectangle, rectangular prism, circle, sphere).

Do: List attributes for each shape (number of sides, number of angles, number of faces).

Lesson: Use different learning modes to gather information about geometric shapes. Students rotate to stations to input new information in various ways.

Choice 1: Walk and Write (Visual, Writing)

Students get a clipboard and go for a walk either around the room or down the hall. Students keep a record in their math journals of the objects they see in the real world and the geometric shapes they resemble (e.g. a sign on the hallway is a rectangle, etc.). Students can also draw geometric shapes and list objects into categories.

Choice 2: Hands-On Identification of Real Objects (Kinesthetic, Writing)

Students are given a set of objects to identify the most similar geometric shape. (Some objects are real world objects such as cereal boxes, balls, etc. as well as math manipulatives.)

Choice 3: Listen and Draw (Auditory, Visual)

Students partner up with one other student, and a privacy divide is put up between the students. One partner has a card with a geometric shape drawn on it. This student must "describe" the shape by stating the attributes to the other partner. The other partner draws his or her prediction of the hidden card. Describer and drawer then compare drawings and switch roles.

Chunk Example 2: States of Matter

C U KAN Lesson Outcomes

Know: The three states of matter (liquid, solid, gas); characteristics of each state (has its own shape, takes on shape of a container, doesn't have a definite shape).

Lesson: This is the first lesson in a unit on states of matter. Students are exploring and gathering information about states of matter. At each station, students will be observing different set of objects. They should keep notes in their science journals about their observations. Ask them to describe the objects at each station by

- Looking at them: What properties do you observe?
- Touching them: What properties do you observe?
- Shaking and listening to them: What properties do you observe?
- Comparing them: What properties do these objects all have in common?

Other Ways to Chunk Information

Auditory: listening
  o tapes, books on tape, lecture, discussion

Kinesthetic: doing, moving, touching, building
  o building, drawing, taking apart, charades, tableau, lab experiment

Visual: seeing, reading, graphing
  o pictures, movies, graphic organizers, conceptual organizers; reading articles, magazines, books

Social: talking, listening, telling others
  o brainstorming, sharing experiences, predicting/hypothesizing, sharing

See Resources for more chunk ideas.

ELEMENT 2: CHEW

*Same information, different ways to **process** new information*

Chew Example 1: Vocabulary Instruction for Different Learning Profiles

C U KAN Lesson Outcomes

Understand: We all learn in different ways; therefore, we need to find ways of studying that work best for our learning style.

Know: Key vocabulary for the unit.

Do: Students choose the best way for themselves individually, as learners, to study vocabulary.

Lesson: These are several lessons that build upon each other for teaching vocabulary in varying ways as you also have each student self-assess and determine which way of studying vocabulary works best for him or her.

In any subject area, new learning is more likely to occur if students comprehend key vocabulary. It is essential that we teach vocabulary in ways that are meaningful to the *variety* of learners in our classrooms. When we were in school, most likely the teacher would have us copy the words and the definitions, memorize them, and then take a test. This strategy worked well for many of us, so we are still using it in our classrooms today. But, as you have probably discovered, the reality is that this strategy works well for *some,* but not *most* of today's learners. Gifted students think that copying and memorizing definitions is a waste of time. They may refuse to do the assignment. Struggling learners spend hours painstakingly copying the words and definitions, but they may not have a clue what they have written! Basically, teaching vocabulary through rote memorization lends itself to input/output learning. Students quickly memorize vocabulary for the test, take the test, and then forget the information shortly thereafter. To teach vocabulary for deep meaning, we need to teach to a variety of learning styles.

Here's another idea we need to keep in mind. Just because textbook publishers bold face words in a text doesn't mean we are required to have students learn them. Textbooks are written for the purpose of selling them to the masses, so they highlight many words. When we try to teach too many key words to students, we will end up doing quantity (input/output) teaching rather than quality (engaging/meaningful) teaching. To determine which words we really need to teach students, we need to look at our curriculum, think about our objectives, and then determine what vocabulary our students most need to know to reach deep understanding of the content. Think about it. We will buy more time to do powerful teaching of vocabulary if we teach five–ten words deeply as opposed to ten–twenty words superficially.

We need to remember that the goal is to help students discover how they learn best. So, as we teach the different approaches for learning vocabulary, we must explain what learning styles the strategies address. Students should be looking for the strategies that work best for them, and they should know to study this way at home as well as in other classes. If we send them out into the world with their own personal tools for making meaning out of new words, we have truly empowered them for a lifetime.

Here are some tried and true ideas for teaching vocabulary in ways that have meaning for all types of learners. Each lesson has a key showing what learning styles we are tapping into when we teach this way.

Learning Style Key   S = See it   W = Write or Draw it   H = Hear it
T = Touch it   M = Move it   Sp = Speak it

1. **Picture Words** (S/T/W): Students draw pictures or graphics that represent vocabulary words. (See Figure 7.3.)

Figure 7.3   Picture Words

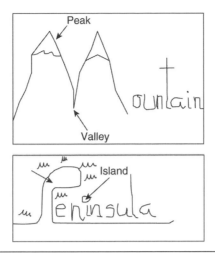

- Fold sheets of 11 x 14 white construction paper into squares and have students draw a picture on each square. Rachel, a student with special needs who loved this strategy, suggested cutting the picture words into squares and then writing the words and descriptions of the words on the back, thus creating study flash cards. Great idea!
- Have students make booklets of vocabulary drawings.
- Using chart paper, put students in groups of three, and give them one word to draw a representation for, then tape the charts around the room and have other students guess which word is represented. Now we're teaching to even more learning styles.

2. **Kiddie Vocabulary** (S/Sp/W): Have students work in pairs to rewrite vocabulary words in ways that a much younger student could understand. For example, here is the eighth grade science word *resistance* with a second grade definition: *When you don't want to do what your mommy wants you to do.*

3. **Vocabulary Bingo** (S/H/Sp/T): This is a great way to review for a test. Have students create their own bingo cards with key vocabulary written on them. Read sentences that leave out the vocabulary. For example, *A ____ economy is based on supply and demand.* Students fill in the vocabulary word on their bingo cards as you read. When a student gets a "bingo," he or she must read the complete sentences for each of the words. In this way, the entire class hears the correct answers each time there is a winner.

4. **Vocabulary Anticipation Guides** (S/H/W): Create true or false sentences about the vocabulary words. Students predict the meaning of each definition by placing a "T" or "F" for each definition. Prepare students to read for meaning and discover the true definitions by looking for context clues and word clues such as prefixes and suffixes and root words. When students read the text assignment, they will be more engaged in the reading as they verify their predictions. After reading the text, go back and discuss the guide and rewrite incorrect answers so that students remember the correct meanings.

5. **Vocabulary Charades** (M/Sp): Put students in groups of two or three. Groups should create actions that represent their vocabulary words. Each group performs a charade of these vocabulary words for the class to predict.

6. **Matching Cards** (S/T/M/W/Sp): Give students strips of card stock. (Cut three strips out of an 8 1/2 x 11 piece of card stock.) On one half, the students write the vocabulary word, and, on the other half, they write definitions in their own words. Then students make their cards into puzzle-like pieces by cutting the cards in half with patterns such as zigzags, curves, or true puzzle shapes. Students can exchange card sets to study from another student's set, or they can quiz each other. (See Figure 7.4.)

Figure 7.4   Vocabulary Matching Cards

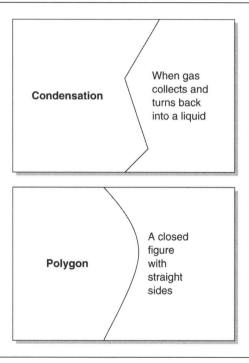

7. **Vocabulary Learning Stations** (S/H/M/W/T/Sp): Set up three to four different learning stations with a different vocabulary strategy at each station (for example, vocabulary pictures, vocabulary charades, and matching cards). Students rotate though the stations in groups. Be sure to ask students which strategies work best for their learning styles.

8. **Ball Toss** (S/H/M/Sp): Have students sit on their desks. Put a vocabulary word on the overhead. Toss a Nerf or Koosh ball to a student, and ask for the meaning of the word. If the student can give you the definition, he or she throws the ball to the next student. If the student doesn't know the word, he or she returns the ball to you to select another student. Repeat!

9. **Moving Matching Cards** (S/H/M/Sp): Using a stack of index cards, write vocabulary words on some cards and the matching definition on others. Shuffle the cards. Pass out one card to each student. Students must move around the room silently to find people with cards that match their own. Students line up around the room with their matches. Replay as time allows.

Chew Example 2: Meaning and Function of Division

C U KAN Lesson Outcomes

Know: Division is related to subtraction and multiplication.

Do: Steps for dividing two numbers.

Lesson: After listening to a demonstration about division and seeing examples done by the teacher, students choose a way to process the information.

Choice 1: Process Through Writing, Analytical Task

Students can be given a prompt such as the following: "Your friend needs a really clear, step-by-step explanation of what division is and how it works. Please write that explanation and help your friend understand division by using number examples as well as words."

Choice 2: Process Through Drawing, Practical Task

Students can show how someone at school, at home, or in the community uses division as part of his daily life. Students can help one another see how and why the person uses division, and give number examples to go along with their illustrations.

Choice 3: Process Visually, Creative Task

Students can be challenged to find a brand new, unique way to help the class see what division is all about and how it works. They can use numbers, visual representations, and/or words to illustrate their ideas so the class is sure to understand.

Other Ways to Chew

Auditory: listening
   o tapes, books on tape, lecture, discussion

Kinesthetic: doing, moving, touching, building
   o building, drawing, taking apart, charades, tableau, lab experiment

Visual: seeing, reading, graphing
   o pictures, movies, graphic organizers, conceptual organizers; reading articles, magazines, books

Social: talking, listening, telling others

o brainstorming, sharing experiences, predicting/hypothesizing, sharing

If you have collected processing style preferences about your students, you can use the following prompts to help students process in a way that is aligned to their learning style:

Practical Applications: Give us an example of . . . How does ___ relate to ___? What is the connection between___ and ___? Make a connection between ___ and ___. Why would this matter to ____? How would ____ use this in his/her (job, life, etc.)? Think of a practical use or application. How does this connect with why you already know?

Creative Applications: What is another way you could show this? What are new, different, or unusual materials you could use to___? What is a new and better way to ___? Develop a conversation that might take place between ____and ____. Develop a (logo, icon, symbol) that represents ____.

Analytical Application: What are the parts that make up . . . ? What are the steps you would take? Where would you start? Explain how __ works. How does it break down? Draw a diagram . . . Record your steps . . . Identify the steps . . . Find parts of components . . .

ELEMENT 3: CHECK

*Same learning target, different ways to **output** or show learning*

Check Example 1: Learning Profile Projects

C U KAN Lesson Outcomes

Understand: Learners use their learning strengths to help them lock in or process information.

Know: Steps of a process (scientific method and/or reducing fractions).

Able To Do: Apply learning strengths to create a mnemonic, or memory trick, for memorizing the steps of a process.

Lesson: Memory Mnemonics

Note: when grouping students for learning profile projects, we can group them by the same or similar learning profiles, allowing students to grow their skills with others who have similar strengths. We can also group students by varied learning profiles to give students an opportunity to have their skills complemented or to create projects that are more multifaceted. The activities that follow are design for students grouped with others who have similar learning profiles.

Scientific Method Mnemonics

Form groups of three students according to students' strongest intelligence. Each group should create a memory trick that would assist someone with their intelligence strength in remembering the steps of the scientific method. Groups will share their creations with the rest of the class.

The Steps of the Scientific Method

- Problem (purpose)
- Hypothesis (because)
- Experiment (test)
- Analyze (think numbers!)
- Conclude

EXPECTATIONS	Bill Nye is jealous!	Pretty good!	Not bad, but no prize	Dr. Science, you are not
Quality (As defined by YOU!) Points: 10	Top Quality 9–10	Good Quality 7–8	Fair Quality 5–6	Needs Better Quality 0–4
Represented all steps of scientific method in a creative way Points: 30	All steps are there and very creative 25–30	All steps are there and rather creative 20–25	Steps missing and minimal creativity 15–20	Steps missing and little creativity 10–15
Used time wisely and worked well in your group Points: 10	Superb 9–10	Standard 7–8	So-so 5–6	Slipped 0–4
What we did that was quality work	What we would do differently next time			

Student Grade _____   Teacher Grade _____

Teacher Comments:

Adding Fractions Mnemonics

Form groups of three students according to students' strongest intelligence. Each group should create a memory trick that would assist someone with their intelligence strength in remembering the steps of adding fractions. Groups will share their creations with the rest of the class.

The Steps of Adding Fractions

- Find the **common denominator**.
- To do that, find the **lowest common multiple** (if all else fails, simply multiply the two denominators together).
- Now, make the two fractions **equivalent fractions**.
- Add the **numerators**.
- Simplify the fraction.

Adding Fractions Mnemonic Rubric

EXPECTATIONS	Great job!	Pretty good!	Not bad, but no prize	Not so hot
Quality (As defined by YOU!) Points:	Top Quality _____	Good Quality _____	Fair Quality _____	Needs Better Quality _____
Showed all steps of adding fractions method in a creative way Points:	All steps are there and very creative _____	All steps are there and rather creative _____	Steps missing and minimal creativity _____	Steps missing and little creativity _____
Used time wisely and worked well in your group Points:	Superb _____	Standard _____	So-so _____	Slipped _____
What we did that was quality work	What we would do differently next time			

Student Grade _____   Teacher Grade _____

Teacher Comments:

Other Ways to Check

Any product a student uses to demonstrate learning should be taken into account by the teacher according to output strengths. We like to use Gardener's Multiple Intelligences as check styles because they take into account students' talents and allow them to express themselves. Remember, same learning target, different ways to show that they get the big idea!

Picture Smart: Mind maps, graphic organizers, videos, color coding, highlighting, shape a word, study illustrations, make a chart, create a poster, create a collage, draw a web, create a cartoon

Word Smart: Write it, tell it, recall it, use "you" words, chunk information, say it, create word mnemonics, write a poem

Music Smart: Sing it, create a beat, rap it, make a cheer, create a jingle, hum it, identify sounds, listen to sounds, connect to music, write a poem

People Smart: Group project, debate, participate in class meeting, do a role play, tutor or teach someone else

Body Smart (sports/acting/etc): Role play, dance, lip sync, do skits/charades/mimes, build it, math manipulatives, use body language

Self Smart: Work alone, solve in your own way, journal it, rehearse it, use what you already know, connect it to yourself, set goals for yourself, show it in your own way

Nature Smart: Make a detailed list, label it, categorize it, identify it, form a prediction, do an experiment, change it, build it, order it, investigate it, look for patterns

Tips for Chunk, Chew, and Check

- Have kids chew often. Keep the new information limited and focused, then have students chew.
- Lessons may be a series of chunk and chew, chunk and chew, chunk and chew before you check. The key is to keep students processing and connecting information.
- The check can be informative data about where to go next with your teaching. It doesn't always have to be formal, summative, and/or graded.
- Sometimes chunk and chew will blend together. The important thing to remember is we don't go from chunk to check. Input/output learning doesn't stick if it isn't chewed on!

 ## ELEMENT 4: CONTENT

*Same learning target, different levels of **complexity** or by the **personal interests** of the students*

Note: As teachers, we live this reality every day. In an ideal world, all students in one grade or class would read at the same level. But this is an unrealistic and unfair view of how the world should be. When would we expect all seven-year-old students to sing equally as well? Why would we expect all twelve-year-olds to grow physically to equal heights? Yet reading, or the linguistic intelligence, is sometimes viewed as a talent that should come equally as easily for all students. What do we do as teachers to meet the needs of these students who are just plain different from one another?

It is essential that we have texts available at various levels, such as textbooks, short essays, and magazine and informational articles related to lessons. You are most likely thinking, "Where am I supposed to get the money and time to supply my class with varying texts?" First, give yourself some time. After the examples, we will give you some suggestions for how to begin collecting varying texts.

Content Example 1: Varying Text Level Investigations

C U KAN Lesson Outcomes

Understand: Heredity determines certain physical characteristics of living things.

Know: Key vocabulary (heredity, genetics, traits, life cycle, metamorphosis).

Able To Do: Compare three living things with different life cycles to determine the impact of genetics.

Lesson: Students will have one essential question to drive their investigations, but will read and analyze varying levels of text to find information. The texts are assigned by the teacher according to their readiness.

The Secret Code of Living Things

Question: What proof can you provide that heredity plays a part in the genetic imprint of all living things?

Task: Your group will be assigned a set of resources to explore. You must look for proof among three living things, with different life cycles, that heredity plays a part in passing down a genetic code. Each person must present his or her own proof but you may share and discuss resources to support your findings. If you need additional resources, please see the teacher.

Content Example 2: Interest-Based Projects

C U KAN Lesson Outcomes

Able To Do: Conduct research and conclude findings to share with community.

Lesson: Students will work in interest-based groups created from a preassessment (see Resources). Groups will become experts in their area and will be called upon throughout the unit to add bits of knowledge and expertise to class discussions. Each group then shares with the rest of the class what its members have learned. Some examples of interest-based groups in content areas might include the following:
- Science
  - Endangered Species—group by the species they are most interested in studying.

- o Simple Machines—students group by the simple machine they are interested in exploring.
- History/Geography
  - o Colonial America—students do an in-depth study of a group of colonists of their choice: Indians, British, the Colonists.
  - o Geography—when students are studying regions, let them become experts in regions that they most want to explore.
- Language Arts/English
  - o Literary Circles—students do "book club" literary circles around books they have selected. You could also teach a literary concept such as internal conflict by letting students find examples in stories that they select to read in interest groups.
  - o Writing Genres—let students create magazines or newsletters by collaborating in groups based on the genre of writing they would like to do (e.g., feature story, advice column, recipes, editorials, etc.).
- Math
  - o Geometry—students work in interest-based groups to study shapes of their choice.
  - o Time—students work in groups to brainstorm activities that can be done in different units of time (e.g., minute, hour, or day).
- Health/Physical Education
  - o Health Awareness—students collaborate in groups around teenage health topics of interest.
  - o Personal Fitness—students have days when they can group together to do fitness activities of their choice (e.g., weight lifting, aerobics, jogging/walking, basketball, etc.).

How to Get Started Collecting Texts of Varying Levels

- Begin with a topic that seems most difficult for students of varying abilities to understand. If we add one or two resource options for this topic every year, our collection will add up quickly.
- With permission, keep papers written by students. Add these to the collection of resource material for a topic.
- Do an Internet search for the topic that needs additional support. Add "children" or "elementary" to your search for information written at less complex levels. The Internet is also a great way to find information for more advanced students.
- Call a local library and have librarians pull resources on your topic.
- If your building has a classroom wish list for the PTA or back to school time, add the resources to this list.
- See the Resources for a list of publishers that offer high interest/low level texts for content area instruction.
- Ask your special education staff or gifted/talented coordinator for ideas and resources.

ELEMENT 5: ENVIRONMENT

*Same learning target, different **space** or different **tone** to meet the learning objective*

Unlike other elements that can be address through specific lessons, the environment is a more constant element that must be differentiated based on students' needs.

Unlike other elements that teachers can address through specific lessons, teachers need to be thoughtful in differentiating the environment in a more consistent way based on students' needs. So, for this section, we offer tips and suggestions for ongoing ways to build a differentiated environment, rather than specific lessons.

Environment Example 1: Routines

Students are allowed choices of work locations that increase their attention and meet their physical needs:

- when taking a test
- when writing or reading
- when listening to a story
- when taking notes

*"I want you to do your very best on this assessment. If you feel you work the best in a location other than a table and chair, you may find a **private** space that is comfortable for you and will help you do your best. We are going to move to our private spaces in a minute, but first gather all your materials and point in the direction you are planning on heading. If you see someone else pointing there, select another location. You will have a slow count of five to quietly move you and your things to your private spot. Oh, and remember, if I see that you might not be doing your best, I have the right to move you to another space that I feel will help you be the best learner that you can be, so choose wisely!"*

Environment Example 2: Group Work

- Teachers give reasons why varied groups are assigned to work together for varied purposes.

"In order to help each other grow, you are going to be working with a group of students who are ready to learn the same information. Based on the pretest, I've made some groups that have similar readiness. Listen for your names."

"For this task, we need lots of different skills: drawing, writing, big picture people, creative people, and people to analyze our steps. To make our projects the best they can be, we need use each other's talents."

- When moving in and out of groups, students have jobs and are responsible for the function of their classroom. If things go wrong, other classmates are used as models to support the growth of those who need more practice.

"Let's take a look at the [science] supplies today. Which group did an excellent job placing their materials back in the science kit? [Students answer group 5] I agree, looks pretty organized. Group 5, would you

mind sharing a few pointers with us? How did you get everything organized so quickly? Perhaps you could show us your secrets of success?"

Environment Example 3: Emotional Tone

- Students' strengths are recognized and often referred to during activities or lessons in order to help them understand themselves as learners and help them continue to grow.
- The relationships within the community are focused on, using each person's skill to help one another grow, not compete against one another.

> *"Now for today's math assignment, we are actually going to need the support of the Art Smart people. Would you raise your hand again if that is your strength? Class, take a look at the other students who can be your helpers if you get stuck with today's graphing."*

- Risk taking and mistake making are encouraged and modeled by the teacher.

> *"As you all know, I'm not a very Music Smart person! But I do know that the brain stores songs very well and it's a great way to remember facts. So, I'm going to sing a song to you today about how rocks are formed. Then we are going to practice it with some movements to help us remember."*

- Music is used to help perk up sluggish students or settle down rowdy ones.
- Brain breaks are used to help students remain engaged and get the wiggles out.
- Lighting is used to increase alertness or create a sense of calm focus.

> *"It sounds like lunch was pretty exciting today. How about we get our brains ready to learn by turning off the lights and listening to some relaxing music for one minute? You can sit with your head on your desk, or relax on the floor while we get ready for relaxed, easy learning!"*
>
> *"Does anyone else here feel that we are a little sluggish today? We know our brains work best with oxygen. Let's do some movement for two minutes to get our brains activated and ready! Tony, will you lead the brain break movements for today while I put on some music?"*

LOOKING AHEAD TO DEEP-N-DYNAMIC DESIGNS

In Chapters 8–13, we will look at how to use small lessons, like the ones you have practiced, come together into unit long "deep-n-dynamic designs" that will allow you to meet state standards and benchmarks.

In these chapters you will see the following:

- a teacher overview to help you understand the design
- "lite-n-lean" ways to get the principles of this design started in your class
- examples of deep-n-dynamic designs written by real classroom teachers

The designs will have a guide to help you understand which component you are looking at within the unit:

- planning guides
- student handouts
- assessments
- rubrics
- a combination of the above components

Once you have developed the C U KAN framework for a lesson, you can decide which deep-n-dynamic design (see Figure 7.5) will have the most benefit for the learning outcomes.

Figure 7.5   Deep-n-Dynamic Designs and the Benefits of Each

Deep-n-Dynamic Designs	Benefits
#1: **Choice Menus**	Engage students based on interests and learning profile Teach students to make choices Use for a variety of purposes (homework, class work, tests)
#2: **RAFT Plus**	Engage through students' interests and learning profiles Teach students to think from other perspectives
#3: **Tiered Lessons**	Engage students based on their readiness level Teach students to be realistic about their readiness to learn new content Challenge students at appropriate readiness levels
#4: **Contracts**	Engage students through learning profiles, interests, and/or readiness levels Teach students accountability Promote independent learning
#5: **Learning Stations**	Engage students through learning profiles, interests, and/or readiness levels Teach students responsibility Use as exploratory or structured
#6: **Compacting**	Engage advanced learners independently Teach advanced learners to take risks

Let's get started with deep-n-dynamic designs.

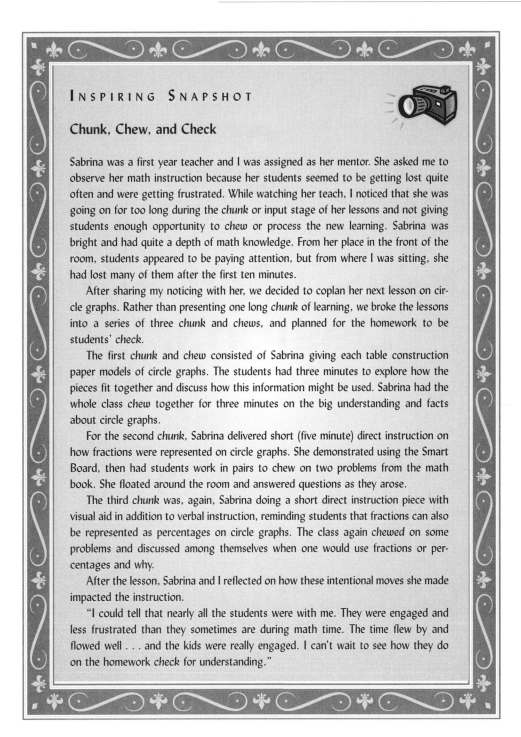

INSPIRING SNAPSHOT

Chunk, Chew, and Check

Sabrina was a first year teacher and I was assigned as her mentor. She asked me to observe her math instruction because her students seemed to be getting lost quite often and were getting frustrated. While watching her teach, I noticed that she was going on for too long during the *chunk* or input stage of her lessons and not giving students enough opportunity to *chew* or process the new learning. Sabrina was bright and had quite a depth of math knowledge. From her place in the front of the room, students appeared to be paying attention, but from where I was sitting, she had lost many of them after the first ten minutes.

After sharing my noticing with her, we decided to coplan her next lesson on circle graphs. Rather than presenting one long *chunk* of learning, we broke the lessons into a series of three *chunk* and *chews*, and planned for the homework to be students' *check*.

The first *chunk* and *chew* consisted of Sabrina giving each table construction paper models of circle graphs. The students had three minutes to explore how the pieces fit together and discuss how this information might be used. Sabrina had the whole class *chew* together for three minutes on the big understanding and facts about circle graphs.

For the second *chunk*, Sabrina delivered short (five minute) direct instruction on how fractions were represented on circle graphs. She demonstrated using the Smart Board, then had students work in pairs to chew on two problems from the math book. She floated around the room and answered questions as they arose.

The third *chunk* was, again, Sabrina doing a short direct instruction piece with visual aid in addition to verbal instruction, reminding students that fractions can also be represented as percentages on circle graphs. The class again *chewed* on some problems and discussed among themselves when one would use fractions or percentages and why.

After the lesson, Sabrina and I reflected on how these intentional moves she made impacted the instruction.

"I could tell that nearly all the students were with me. They were engaged and less frustrated than they sometimes are during math time. The time flew by and flowed well . . . and the kids were really engaged. I can't wait to see how they do on the homework *check* for understanding."

8

Deep-n-Dynamic Design #1

Choice Menus

TEACHER OVERVIEW

Concept: Choice menus are about exactly that, the power of "choice."

Understand That (key principles):

- Learners feel more in control of their learning environment and are more engaged, accountable, and responsible when they are given a voice and a choice in their learning.
- Learners must be taught, at age-appropriate levels, how to make choices, how to follow through on their plans, and how to self-assess their progress.

Know (facts):

- Choice menus provide a graphic "menu" of activities for students to select from to show how they have learned objectives of a lesson (C U KAN) or to reinforce learning of a concept. Menus can be based on students' readiness, interest, and/or learning profile. Choices can be offered at the Chunk, Chew, or Check part of a lesson. Choice options can take many forms such as activity menus, dicing, tic-tac-toes, and cubing.

Able To Do (skills):

- The teacher determines the C U KAN that students must know from a unit of study or lesson.
- The teacher creates a graphic menu or list of options for demonstrating what students must show they've learned. (average two–six items at elementary level)
- Menu options can be created according to students' readiness level, interest, or learning profile.
- Students choose their menu options and record choices.
- Rubrics may be designed for student self-assessment and teacher assessment.

Now You Get It!

- Choice designs:
  o promote appropriate challenges for all learners
  o provide opportunities for success for all students
  o provide respectful and relevant learning activities for all students
  o allow for students to be more actively engaged in their learning process
  o promote students' responsibility, independence, and accountability
  o are highly engaging for students and teachers

LITE-N-LEAN WAYS TO USE CHOICES

One of the easiest ways to honor students' different learning styles is to give them choices. Students respond powerfully when they are able to select how they will share what they learned. You can introduce choice in a variety of ways. We will look at choices on homework, tests, and studying vocabulary.

Choices on Homework

Surface Area Homework Assignment

Students can *choose* from one of the following items, so that they can *best* apply what they have learned in class on the particular day. Tell them it will be due the next day for 10 points.

- Imagine that you have become weightless and can float above your bedroom. Draw a picture of the furniture that you see. Give imaginary dimensions (be sure to use units), and find the area of the floor that is covered by at least three pieces of furniture.
- You have been given the job of taking care of Tweets, the family bird. You must change the newspaper in the bottom of her cage every Saturday. Your environmentally conscious mother does not want any paper wasted. Decide how you would best determine the area

to be covered in the cage. What strategy could you use to make it easy every Saturday?

- Complete problems (for example, "#8–18 on page 256") in Check for Understanding.
- Create a poem describing a beautiful hand woven rug from India and how the weaver could find out the area that it will cover.
- *Choose* one of the above choices, and in a brief paragraph, debate with a friend why a formula is used to determine area instead of counting squares on a grid or using plastic unit tiles.

Choices on Tests

The following choices were given to a fifth grade science class at the end of a subjective test.

Animal Kingdom

Choose one of the following activities below to show what you have learned in this chapter. (5 points each)

- Create an imaginary organism that will fit in one of the kingdoms *except* the animal kingdom. Draw a picture of that organism. Tell what major characteristics it has in order to be placed in the kingdom you chose.
- Write a short letter to an archaeologist describing briefly what you have learned about fossils and geology. Include several questions that you may have developed while studying this chapter that he or she could answer.
- Develop five questions that could appear on the television show, *Are You Smarter Than a Fifth Grader*? They should be about topics that were *not* covered on this test but related to this chapter.
- Create a rhyme that you could teach to a third grade student so that she or he could remember the categories of classification. How would you begin a discussion with third graders about the importance of a classification system? What could you compare that system to in their lives?
- Think about a walk in the woods. List seven things you might encounter, and describe how you would begin to classify them. Be as specific as possible. Choose two of the organisms and describe an adaptation that has enabled them to thrive in their environment.

Choices for Vocabulary

The following menu was given to a class as a way to study vocabulary.

Vocabulary Menu

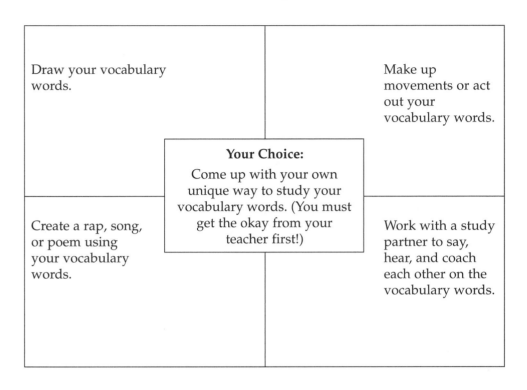

Draw your vocabulary words.

Make up movements or act out your vocabulary words.

Your Choice:
Come up with your own unique way to study your vocabulary words. (You must get the okay from your teacher first!)

Create a rap, song, or poem using your vocabulary words.

Work with a study partner to say, hear, and coach each other on the vocabulary words.

Weekly Vocabulary Choices

Choose your challenge level. Select vocabulary practice activities that equal 30 points for an A, 25 points for a B, and 20 points for a C.

30 points = A   25 points = B   20 points = C

- ❑ Make a set of flash cards for studying your words. (10 pts)
- ❑ Practice reviewing the words and their meanings with a family member or friend. (5 pts)
- ❑ Create a song or rhyme for each vocabulary word. (15 pts)
- ❑ Draw a picture that shows your understanding of each word. (15 pts)
- ❑ Write sentences that show you understand the meaning of each word. Underline the word. (10 pts)
- ❑ Use a tape recorder to practice words. State each word, give the definition, and then spell it. (10 pts)
- ❑ Create a word game (bingo, word search, crossword, charades, or make fill-ins). (15 pts)
- ❑ Create a word wall bulletin board with descriptions of each word. (15pts)
- ❑ Classify the words according to the parts of speech (grammar books are available). (10 pts)

(Continued)

(Continued)

- ❑ Write a story using all the words (correct paragraph format). Underline the vocabulary words. (15 pts)
- ❑ Write a synony and an antonym for each word. (15 pts)
- ❑ Use your words in poetry. Underline the words. (15 pts)
- ❑ Write newspaper headlines using your words. (15 pts)
- ❑ Create a word map for each word. Use at least four categories. (If you include a description of the word, then you can count that as your 15 points for describing the word. See list of map ideas.) (15–30 pts)
- ❑ Create your own activity. (15 pts) (Ask for approval from the teacher.)

Choices on Vocabulary Maps

Mapping is an excellent strategy for learning vocabulary. Vocabulary maps allow students to explore a word in various ways. Students can create their own vocabulary maps, or they can work with a partner or small group to create maps. Have students keep a vocabulary journal in a spiral notebook or composition book. This will give students a log of their vocabulary learning and will also keep you away from the copy machine!

Groups can create a map for different words and then teach each other their words using their maps. Keep the maps posted in the room so that students can keep learning from them. Teachers can assign one or two "Must Do" categories and then allow students to choose two categories of their own. Some categories for vocabulary mapping may include the following (teachers should select several categories that are appropriate for the age and subject level they are teaching):

- guess the meaning (prefixes, suffixes, root words)
- what is it/describe the word
- antonyms/opposite words
- synonyms/related words
- analogies/similes/metaphors ("This is like . . . ")
- examples from text (number problems, experiments, etc.)
- examples from life
- examples from TV/movies
- use of words in sentence
- connections to related concepts
- pictures/drawing

Figure 8.1   Vocabulary Maps

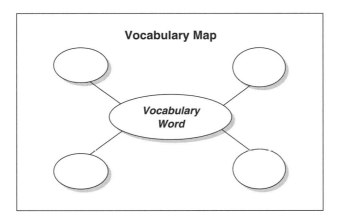

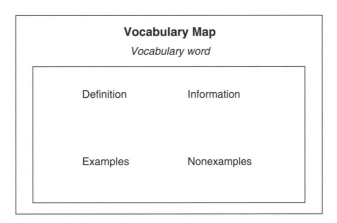

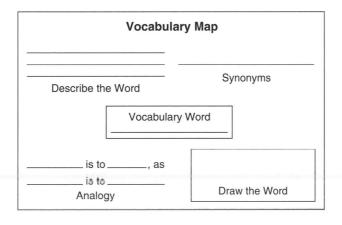

DEEP-N-DYNAMIC DESIGNS FOR USING CHOICES

First Grade Math

Subject: First Grade Math

Design: Choice Menu

Lesson Component: Learning Target and Student Handout

Understanding Time

Understand That: People created time to help us organize our day.

Know: Hour, Half Hour, Half-Past

Able To Do: Tell time to the hour and half hour

Now You Get It: Choose something from the menu and show what you know about time.

Draw a picture that shows what you know about telling time in hours and half hours. Write words or a story about a person who has trouble with time to go with your drawing. 	Make up a song or a rhythm about telling time in hours and half hours.
Make a story about your day and time. Act out your story. Be sure to use hours and half hours in your story. 	Make a chart of your favorite TV shows and what time they start. Use hours and half hours.

Subject: First Grade Math

Design: Choice Menu

Lesson Component: Student Rubric

Understanding Time Rubric

Name: _____

Project Choice:_____

HOW I DID	😊	☹
I understand that time helps me organize my life.		
I can tell time by hour and half hour.		
I did quality work.		

What I did that I am really proud of doing . . .

_____

What I could do better next time . . .

_____

Teacher comments:

Third Grade Social Studies

Subject: Third Grade Social Studies

Design: Choice Menu

Lesson Component: Learning Target, Student Handout, and Rubric

My Community Menu

Concept: Interactions

Understand That: Communities are made up of interactions between humans and their environment.

Know: Facts about your community

Able To Do: Gather data and record it in a data table

Write a story about your family's interaction with your community.	Write an article for the school or local newspaper about your interaction with your community.
Write out note cards and do an oral presentation (with artifacts) about you and your interactions with your community.	Write a letter to your pen pal about you and your interactions with your community.

Your Choice:
Come up with your own unique writing way to show how you interact with your community. (You must get the okay from your teacher first!)

Subject: Third Grade Social Studies

Design: Choice Menu

Lesson Component: Student Rubric

My Community Rubric

What We Learned	Made It!	Almost There!	On Your Way	Getting Started
Understand that people interact with nature and each other in a community				
Describe favorite human and environmental characteristics of your community				
Quality Work (As defined by you!)				

Ways I Will Do Quality Work on My Project:

1. _____

2. _____

Fourth Grade Science

Subject: Fourth Grade Science

Design: Choice Menu

Lesson Component: Learning Target, Student Handout, and Rubric

Scientific Investigation

Concept: Process

Understand That: Scientists use a process to explore questions and draw conclusions.

Know:

- Scientific questions can be tested and data can be observed and collected.
- Variable, analysis, hypothesis, types of simple machines: screw, pulley, level, inclined plane, wedge, wheel, and axel.

Able To Do:

- Design an investigation, gather data, analyze data, make a conclusion using evidence

After weeks of studying simple machines the class conducted an investigation with one of the simple machines as a whole class. They came up with the question, "Does the size of a wheel affect the distance a vehicle travels?"

As a class they next assigned roles for gathering materials and collecting data. One group brainstormed "things that could give us bad data." They came to a whole class conclusion that it was essential to only test one variable—wheel size. Because of this, the class decided to assign one person to be the "pusher" because it would reduce the variables. After doing one investigation as a class and collecting data on a shared investigation form on the overhead, they brainstormed other scientific questions that could be investigated. The kids were excited and anxious to do their own.

Note: The Know of this lesson, the key terms, was assessed during the weeks of studying the unit, so the teacher did not include the Know in the final rubric for this project.

Subject: Fourth Grade Science

Design: Choice Menu

Lesson Component: Student Handout

Name: _____ Date: _____

Directions:

As a group, choose one question from the "I wonder" board to investigate. Maintain investigation records that include the essential steps below. Prepare to share your findings with your scientific community. Make sure you describe the *considerations you made to make sure you were testing only one variable.*

I wonder

If we put three wheels on a vehicle, will it travel farther than if it had two wheels?

Will it go faster with more wheels?

Will the tire material affect the distance a vehicle travels?

Will it go faster with smoother tires than with tires that have ridges?

Does the size of the axel affect the distance a vehicle will travel?

Does the length of the axel affect the speed?

Steps for Investigations

Question for our investigation:

What we think the answer to our question will be (hypothesis):

Materials we will need to test our answer:

Procedures for our investigation:

Observations:

Summary of our results:

What we learned (conclusion):

Scientific explanation for conclusion:

Possible errors in our investigation:

Additional questions I could investigate related to this question.

Subject: Fourth Grade Science

Design: Choice Menu

Lesson Component: Rubric

How I Did	4	3	2	1
Understand that scientists follow a process	Shows complex understanding of the concept; explores related ideas	Understands the concept; connects to related ideas	Limited understanding of the key ideas; little elaboration of ideas	Little understanding; no or inaccurate support from data or related ideas
Able to do: Gather data Draw conclusion from data	In depth and well supported with accurate details	Well supported by details	Valid but little depth; no details	Not accurate
Group work/notes	Encourages others; collaborates and resolves conflicts	Listens well, helps others, shares	Appropriate effect; cooperative	Inappropriate effort; not cooperative

Group Reflection

What we did well: _____

_____

_____

How our thinking changed: _____

_____

_____

What we might do/try next time: _____

_____

_____

Group Grade _____   Teacher Grade _____

Fifth Grade English Language Arts

Subject: Fifth Grade English Language Arts

Design: Choice Menu

Lesson Component: Learning Target, Student Handout, and Rubric

Determining Theme

Understand That: Empowered readers seek to make connections from text to life.

Know: Evidence, dialogue, and theme

Able To Do:

Identify the theme/purpose

Support your thinking by finding evidence from the text

Determine important facts from interesting facts

Compare and contrast the theme from two texts

Directions:

Choose a short story to read. Determine the theme of the short story and how it connects to your life. Choose a way that you will demonstrate your understanding of the theme. Some possible choices are listed below.

Product	Intelligence Strength
Write another short story with a similar theme	Logical, linguistic
Act out a skit	Kinesthetic, interpersonal
Draw a cartoon or comic strip	Visual
Write and perform a song/rap	Musical, linguistic
Create a collage	Visual
Write a poem about the theme	Linguistic, musical
Keep a journal of how the theme connects to your life	Intrapersonal
Demonstrate it your own way (your choice)	

(Continued)

(Continued)

How I Did	5	4	3	2	1
Understand that authors write for a purpose					
Know . . . Demonstrate knowledge of terms, dialogue, theme, evidence					
Able To Do: Identify theme Use evidence Make comparison and contrasts					
Quality Work 1. 2.					
Work Habits Used time wisely Organized					

How will I be graded?

Reflections:

The part I liked best about today's assignment was: _____

_____

_____

Next time I: _____

_____

_____

Today I learned: _____

_____

_____

CHOICE DESIGN: TEACHING TIPS

Lesson Design

- It is essential to be clear on the target, or C U KAN objectives, before designing your choices. Then you can make sure you are selecting choice options that match the learning target.
- Before offering students choices (especially in K–2), have everyone in the class do one project type so they know how to do that project type. For example, have the whole class make picture books. For another lesson have them all do a skit. Then the next time, you can give them the choice of picking one of those two projects. As they learn to do more projects, those projects can be added to the choices you give them.
- When starting to give choices, offer fewer choices, especially in the early elementary grades. Keep it simple for your own benefit.
- It helps to give students some examples of what you want them to do. However, don't explain how to do *everything* and don't give them the exact criteria for how to do the projects. When you spell out everything for students, they don't learn how to develop the planning skills on their own. (We've found that elementary students can do way more on their own than we think, when we give them the chance.) If you don't have past student examples to share, try coming up with some simple examples yourself.
- Students can be expected to do only one choice, or several choices on the menu, depending on the time you have and the complexity of the choices.
- Have one of the choices on the menu be, "Your Choice: Must Be Approved by Teacher." Why? Students will come up with amazing ideas when you open the doors for them to do so.
- If you include a choice on your menu that's traditional, for example, "Do page 23 in the book," and most students choose that, next time you do a menu, don't include that choice. If you still want something traditional, but you want to challenge them, have the choice be, "Design a worksheet/test and make an answer key to go along with it."

Management

- Students must do quality work on their product choice. Prior to working on their product, have students write down or share with you specifically how they will do quality work for that project type. (For example, Quality Skit Criteria: We will use costumes, know our parts, and rehearse at least three times. Or, in early elementary, Quality Picture Book Criteria: I used pretty colors, I did my best drawing.) To teach students how to think about defining quality, you can model examples of how to determine what makes a quality project. You will be assessing each student as well as having them assess themselves on the criteria they identified, so you want to teach them to be really specific. See Resources for more ideas on Quality Work.

- Collecting Work
  - Number the menu choices and collect by number. ("All those who did #1, please turn in your posters at this time," etc.)
  - If students will be presenting their projects (skits, songs, etc.), it helps to make an advance sign-up sheet for students who will be presenting. Be very specific on how much presentation time, will be allowed. (Usually, if students ramble on and use too much time, it's because they are not prepared.)

Assessment

- Correct by project type. Correct all the posters, then all the poems, etc. This gets you in the "groove" of the project type.
- Design rubrics that allow for grading different projects types with the same rubric. See the Choice Menu rubric examples in this section.
- Remember, when you first start giving kids choices, some will do an amazing job and some will slop through it. It's a good idea, the first few times you try a menu, to share several products from students who have done quality work, so that the class begins to understand what you are expecting. The more you expect and show them how to reach quality in their work, the more you will begin to see it! (Start keeping examples of "Quality Projects" that students have completed so that you can share them as examples in future classes.)

Teacher Self-Assessment

If students are doing great projects, but they are still missing the target, you need to be sure that the C U KAN is written on the menu and that you keep reminding students that having thorough content and becoming experts is part of the assessment rubric for the project.

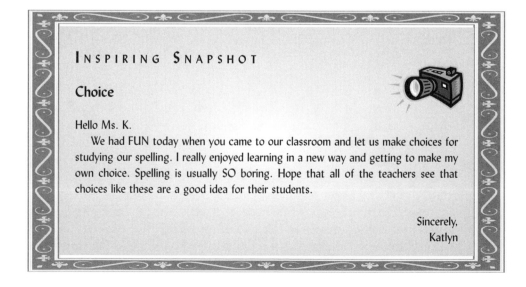

INSPIRING SNAPSHOT

Choice

Hello Ms. K.

We had FUN today when you came to our classroom and let us make choices for studying our spelling. I really enjoyed learning in a new way and getting to make my own choice. Spelling is usually SO boring. Hope that all of the teachers see that choices like these are a good idea for their students.

Sincerely,
Katlyn

9

Deep-n-Dynamic Design #2

RAFT Plus

TEACHER OVERVIEW

Concept: Perspective

Understand That (key principles): Students gain deeper understandings about content if they engage from the perspective of something or someone within that content.

Know (facts): The RAFT format

R = Role (can be animate or inanimate)

A = Audience (someone or something affected by or connected to the role)

F = Format (choices based on learning styles or multiple intelligences)

T = task/learning outcome (the Understand, Know, and Do of your objectives)

Able To Do (skills):

- The teacher determines the outcomes that students must know from a unit of study.
- The teacher creates a few RAFT Plus options for demonstrating what students learn. (3–5 average)

- RAFT Plus options can be tiered, by choice, by interests, or by readiness level.
- Students work independently or in groups to create self-selected projects to show their understanding of concepts studied.
- Teacher and students use rubrics to assess completed products from the RAFT Plus products or projects.

Now You Get It!
RAFT Plus lessons:

- promote student initiative
- provide opportunities for success for all students
- provide learning opportunities that are relevant to students
- allow for students to be more actively engaged in their learning process
- promote students' responsibility, independence, and accountability
- are fun to do!

LITE-N-LEAN WAYS TO USE RAFT PLUS

RAFT Plus for Social Skills

If there social problems occurring in your class, have students practice role-playing solutions by taking on the other person's perspective. For example, if students are teasing, they could practice role play by acting as the person being teased, and explaining to the other student how that makes him or her feel. This is a great way to have students learn empathy and see things from someone else's perspective.

RAFT Plus for Homework

Students can do small RAFT Plus assignments for homework as a way to chew on what they've been learning. Some examples would be . . .

- You are an adverb explaining to verbs how you modify them.
- You are a numerator explaining to a denominator that you represent a part of its whole.
- You are a butterfly explaining to a caterpillar how it will grow up to be just like you some day.

DEEP-N-DYNAMIC DESIGNS FOR USING RAFT PLUS

Kindergarten Spelling

Subject: Kindergarten Spelling

Design: RAFT Plus

Lesson Component: Learning Target and Student Handout

My Letter RAFT

Understand That: Language is made up of patterns. When we know the patterns we can make sense of the language.

Know:

- One pattern in English is the use of capitals and lower case letters.
- The letter "D" or any letter of the alphabet.
- Upper and lower case letters have special purposes.

Able To Do:

- Identify lower and uppercase letters
- Talk and write as you explain the differences between upper and lower case "D"

R = Upper case "D"/Lower case "d" (any letter)

A = Lower case "d"/upper case "D" (the opposite of what you are)

F = Speak and/or write

T = Tell how you are alike and different

- Plan with your partner
- Practice
- Share

Subject: Kindergarten Spelling

Design: RAFT Plus

Lesson Component: Rubric

The Letter "D": Rubric

Name: _____

How I Did	Good	Not So Good
Understands that language has patterns	☺	☹
Knows the difference between "d" and "D"	☺	☹
Good Presentation (Quality Work)	☺	☹

TEACHER COMMENTS:

Second Grade Science

Subject: Second Grade Science

Design: RAFT Plus

Lesson Component: Learning Target and Student Handout

Endangered Species

RAFT Assignment

Role = An Endangered Species: Bald Eagles, Wolf, Polar Bear, Alligator, Gorilla, Panda, Tiger, Elephant, Dolphin, Whale

Audience = Humans

Format = Skit/puppet show, song/rap/poem, brochure, newspaper or magazine, article, children's picture book, your choice (see teacher for okay)

Tasks = Research from your view point and try to persuade society to adopt your viewpoint.

Learning Target

Understand That: Human actions have an effect on other living things

Know:

- Humans can care for and save animals
- Facts about an animal and how to save it from extinction

Able To Do: Research and take notes about your animal. Present your findings *as* that animal.

Subject: Second Grade Science

Design: RAFT Plus

Lesson Component: Student Note-Taking Guide

Endangered Species

RAFT Research Notes

Name: _____ Animal: _____

Where our animal lives	
What our animal eats	
How we can help our animal to NOT become extinct	
Other facts about our animal	

Subject: Second Grade Science

Design: RAFT Plus

Lesson Component: Rubric

Endangered Species Rubric				
Name: _____				
What We Learned	*Great*	*Good*	*Okay*	*Keep Working*
Humans have an effect on other living things				
Know what endangered means Know facts about your animal				
Quality notes				
Quality work (As defined by you!)				

Ways I will do quality work for my project:

_____

_____

What I did that was quality work . . .

What I would do better next time . . .

Third Grade Math

Subject: Third Grade Math

Design: RAFT Plus

Lesson Component: Learning Target and Student Handout

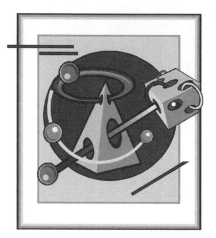

My Shape: RAFT Plus Project

Role = Geometric Shape

Audience = Another shape

Format = Song/poem/rap, children's book letter, skit/speech, your choice (teacher must okay)

Task = What I look like and how I am different from you

Concept: Characteristics

Understand That: People describe and name things so they can communicate about them easily.

Know: Two-dimensional and three-dimensional geometric shapes

Able To Do: Identify geometric shape characteristics and compare and contrast them.

Now You Get It: Create and communicate a way to show how the characteristics of your shape compare to another shape.

Subject: Third Grade Math

Design: RAFT Plus

Lesson Component: Rubric

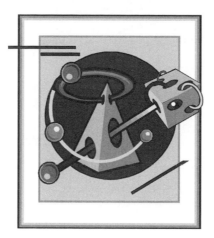

My Shape Rubric				
Name: _____				
What We Learned	*Great*	*Good*	*Okay*	*Keep Working*
Understand that we name things and their characteristics to communicate				
Know and can identify characteristics of shapes				
Quality work (As defined by you!)				
Ways I will do quality work for my project: _____ _____				
What I did that was quality work… What I would do better next time…				

Fifth Grade English Language Arts

Subject: Fifth Grade English Language Arts

Design: RAFT Plus

Lesson Component: Learning Target & Student Handout

Be Yourself: RAFT Plus Project

Role = Star Girl/Camille/Gerald the Giraffe

Audience = Kids Today

Format = Song/poem/rap, comic strip, children's book, motivational speech, public service announcement, your choice (teacher must okay)

Task = Share what this character learned about staying true to one's self and give advice about how to be true to yourself in today's world

Concept: Self

Understand That: Authors create stories that can teach us important things about life and about ourselves.

Know: The character of your story and how that character learned to be true to himself or herself.

Able To Do: Read the story and take notes about the character.

Now You Get It: Create a project from the perspective of one of the characters that shows what you learned about being true to yourself.

Subject: Fifth Grade English Language Arts

Design: RAFT Plus

Lesson Component: Rubric

Be Yourself Rubric

Expectations	Slipped	So-So	Sufficient	Super
Understand that stories can teach us about life and ourselves _____ Pts.				
Describe what your character learned about life _____ Pts.				
Quality Work _____ Pts.				
Used Class Time Wisely _____ Pts.				

Ways I/We Will Do Quality Work for Our Project:

1. _____

2. _____

What I/we did that was quality work …

What I/we would do differently next time …

RAFT PLUS: TEACHING TIPS

Lesson Design

- Develop the C U KAN for the lesson prior to designing the menu. This way you can be sure the RAFT Plus you create meets the objectives of the C U KAN.
- Note to Beginners: When you first try a RAFT, it's okay to have all the students do the same Role, Audience, Format, and Task. As you evolve in your skills, then you can begin giving them more options within the RAFT.
- RAFT Plus can be short-term or long-term assignments (two days or two weeks, homework or class work).
- RAFT Plus can be done alone or in groups.
- Try to offer choices in the RAFT project. You can change the role and the format quite easily. You can assign different roles to different students or have different audiences. For example, half the class could be unionist, the other half confederates, and they could present to each other why they have chosen to be on that side.

Management

- Students must do quality work on their product choice. Once students have picked their project type and have begun working on it, give them the assessment rubric. Note that quality work is one of the expectations on the rubric. At the bottom of the rubric, have students write down at least three criteria that tell *specifically* how they will do quality work for that project type. You will be grading them on the three criteria they identified, so you want them to be really specific.
- Have students develop a plan to show you what they are going to do. If they are working in groups, they must show that they have divided up the tasks so that everyone has a task to do.
- If students will be presenting their projects (skits, songs, etc.) make an advance sign-up sheet for students who need to present. Be very specific on how much presentation time will be allowed. (Usually, if students ramble on and use too much time, it's because they are not prepared.)
- If you're doing a more long-term project, have students become "experts" before they work on the creative part of the project. This is a good time to have them work on foundational skills like note-taking or graphic organizers. Once they show you that they have the content knowledge, they can work on the project.
- While students are working on their choices, be sure to float around the room and check to see that they have the Understand, Know, and Able To Do in their project.

Assessment

- The rubric has Understand, Know, Quality Work, and whatever other category you may choose to assess.
- Always have students assess themselves on their projects first. Then you assess using the same rubric.
- Remember that when you first start giving kids RAFT Plus, some will do an amazing job and some will slop through it. It's a good idea, the first few times you try a RAFT Plus, to share several products of students who have done quality work, so that the class begins to understand what you are expecting. The more you expect and show them how to reach quality in their work, the more you will begin to see it!

Teacher Self-Assessment

As you try out RAFT Plus, note what's working and what is not. Keep doing what *is* working, and troubleshoot what's not. For example, if students have found great content, but aren't really stepping into the role, you may have to model a few examples of "becoming" someone, or something else to help them see what you are expecting.

If you are using RAFT Plus as a group project:

- Assign students in groups by choice, readiness, or learning profile. (If you assign groups by readiness, you can easily tier the assignment.)
- Have the students choose their jobs in the group. (Some jobs could be leader, scribe, teacher-getter, organizer, time keeper, life coach.) Be sure to have the students be responsible for their jobs.
- As a class, discuss appropriate group behaviors. Design a group behavior rubric based on their discussions.
- Talk about the consequences of not working with the group. If a person chooses to hurt and not help the group, they can get "fired" from the group and have to work on an independent activity.
- Have the groups self-assess at the end of each work session. Then you, as their "boss," agree or disagree with their assessment.

I N S P I R I N G   S N A P S H O T

RAFT Plus

(The students did such a great job on this RAFT assignment the teacher had some of them printed in the local paper.)

Dear Pet Owners,

Hi, My name is Henry and I am a kitten. I am in the animal shelter because no one took care of me. I am very scared here because I don't know very many animals.

I am also scared of dying. That's what will happen to me if no one takes me home. I get very lonely and sad because I have nobody to cuddle with. I feel sick and dirty because there aren't enough people here to keep all of us clean. When people walk by my cage, I get very excited because I think they are going to take me home. But, they pass me by and forget about me and I feel very disappointed. I don't like living in the shelter.

You can keep your animals out of the shelter. You should keep your pets inside or put a collar with identification on them so they don't get lost or stolen. Take care of your pets by giving them food, shelter, warmth, medical care, and love. If you can't take care of more than one animal then get your pet spayed or neutered.

An animal shelter is a horrible place to live. Take care of your pets so they don't end up like me.

Yours Truly,
Henry

10

Deep-n-Dynamic Design #3

Tiered Lessons

TEACHER OVERVIEW

Concept: Readiness

Understand That (key principles): Learners must have a challenge that is appropriate for them in order for learning to occur. Students experience more success when learning occurs at the level of challenge that is appropriate for them.

Know (facts): In a mixed ability classroom, the teacher develops lessons at varying levels based on the same curriculum concept (essential idea) so that students may experience the learning at their appropriate ability level.

Able To Do (skills):

- The teacher determines the basic concepts that students must understand, know, and do from a unit of study.
- The teacher preassesses to find background knowledge of students for that unit of study.
- Based on the preassessment, the teacher decides how many tiers of learning need to be developed.

- The teacher develops meaningful and respectful tasks for each tier of learners to accomplish.
- The teacher plans anchor activities for students to work on if the teacher is explaining to other groups or if students finish work early.
- The teacher develops authentic assessment tools to assess student learning at all tiers.

Now You Get It!
Tiered lessons:

- promote appropriate challenge for all learners
- provide opportunities for success for all students
- provide respectful and relevant learning activities for all students
- allow for students to be more actively engaged in their learning process
- promote students' responsibility, independence, and accountability

LITE-N-LEAN WAYS TO TIER

By simply thinking about the varying levels of readiness in our classroom, we can begin to think of simple ways to respond to our students' academic diversity. Below are some easy ways to vary the difficulty levels of an assignment or activity for your students.

Tiering Homework

Rather than giving everyone the same homework, we can give leveled homework assignments. We can assign students the difficulty level we think they need or let them choose the level that they feel is right for them. For example, in math we can assign Homework Assignment A, B, or C to students as the homework assignment that best meets their needs. Color coding the homework assignments (pink, yellow, blue) helps us see the different tiers more easily.

Tiering Questions

Another simple way we can tier is to ask students questions at varying levels of complexity. Students can respond to these questions as part of classroom discussions or as written responses. When tiering by question complexity, it's important to remember to offer students a variety of questions at different levels of Bloom's taxonomy in order to start where they are ready but also stretch their thinking. (See Resources for Bloom's Taxonomy Question Starters.)

Tiering With Your Textbook

Many textbooks today build in activities for reteaching and enriching students' learning. We can use these ready-made pages to help students who need additional practice or to challenge students who already get it!

Tiering Vocabulary

When tiering vocabulary, we can determine key vocabulary that is essential to student understanding of a topic. We then preassess to see which words students already know. We can us this data to begin grouping our students. If there are words that none of our students know, we can teach those words as a whole class. Looking at the remainder of the vocabulary terms, we can group students into (a) students who don't know all the remaining words and (b) students who know all the remaining words. We can have students who still need to learn key words use quality vocabulary techniques to learn these words. Students who already know the remaining key words can study more advanced words in the content that aren't "need to know" words, but are words that will take their thinking deeper.

On-the-Spot Flexible Grouping

If we are good kid watchers, we can see the need to do on-the-spot flexible grouping. For example, as we are teaching a lesson, we make a point to notice our students' facial expressions and body language. If we have students who are nodding away at us—indicating, "Yes, I get it!"— then we may want to pull them together and offer them a challenge option. This will engage these learners where they need to be engaged, and will give us a chance to pull together the students who are looking at us in total confusion. We can also teach our students to self-assess and self-tier. After we teach a lesson, we can say to students, "If this is really easy for you, come to me and I will give you something more challenging to do. If you need some extra help on this, come back to the table with me and we will go over it again." You will be amazed at how many students will self-select the appropriate learning challenge for themselves.

DEEP-N-DYNAMIC DESIGNS FOR TIERING

Kindergarten Math

Subject: Kindergarten Math

Design: Tiered Lessons

Lesson Component: Learning Target and Student Handout

Understand That: Patterns are specific, predictable, continuous, and observable in our environment. Mathematicians use patterns to organize information for use in problem solving.

Know (facts): Numbers 10, 20, 30, 40, 50, 60, 70, 80, 90, 100

Able To Do (skills): Count to 100 by 10s using task cards

- Group items into groups of 10 to help with counting
- Write numbers 10, 20, 30, 40, 50, 60, 70, 80, 90, 100

Preassess by having students individually try counting to 100 by 10s and/or having them write the numbers used to count to 100 by 10s.

Tier 1: Materials/Content

10 20
30 40

Use popsicle sticks to make groups of 10. Bundle the groups of 10 with a rubber band, and keep making groups until you get to 100. How many groups of 10 do you need?

Tier 2: Materials/Content

10 20
30 40

Draw a picture of an object of your choice (sticks, balls, or Xs). Circle every group of 10 until you get to 100. How many groups do you have? What tools could you use if you are having trouble?

Tier 3: Materials/Content

10 20
30 40

Choose one of the following:

- Create a 100s chart of your own.
- Write addition problems using groups of 10s.
- Make up a song about counting by 10s.

Assessment

Name: _____

I thought my task card was too hard.

I thought my task card was too easy.

Place the numbers that you use to count to 100 in the box.

SOURCE: Lesson contributed by Jenna Blair, Melissa Foster, and Angela Kiryakza.

Third Grade Language Arts, Spelling

Subject: Third Grade Language Arts, Spelling

Design: Tiered Lessons

Lesson Component: Learning Target and Lesson

Understand That (key principles): Examining words helps us find patterns and consistencies that will help us solve unknown words. Finding patterns will also help us when we are asked to spell unknown words.

Know (facts): Students will learn that words in the English language often are spelled based on patterns. By studying and learning these patterns, we will increase our word recognition, knowledge about spelling, and meaning of words.

Able To Do (skills): Recognize different spelling patterns within the English language and be able to transfer that knowledge to help solve and spell words during reading and writing workshop.

Tier 1: Materials/Content

Students will sort words by ending sounds based on the word families ick, ack, and uck. Next, they will rewrite their words into "ack" sound, "ick" sound, and "uck" sound families in their word study notebook. Finally, they will go on a word hunt through their independent reading book, adding words as they fit into these families. On a separate sheet of paper, students will make a list of these words and will write a short paragraph explaining the pattern they were looking for and why it's important to notice word patterns.

Tier 2: Materials/Content

Students will sort their words based on short and long "u" vowel sound. Next, they will rewrite their words into short "u" sound, long "u" sound, and oddball categories in their word study notebook. Finally, they will go on a word hunt through their independent reading book, adding words as they fit into the categories. On a separate sheet of paper, students will make a list of these words and will write a short paragraph explaining the pattern they were looking for and why it's important to notice word patterns.

Tier 3: Materials/Content

Students will sort their words based on short and long vowel sounds (their words include all the vowels). Next, in their word study notebook, students will divide a page into three sections and go on a word hunt through their independent reading book, adding words as they fit into the categories. On a separate sheet of paper, students will make a list of these words and will write a short paragraph explaining the pattern they were looking for and why it's important to notice word patterns.

(Continued)

(Continued)

Spelling Rubric

Expectations	Great ☺	Good	Okay	Not So Good ☹
Understand: That words have patterns _____ Pts				
Know: The pattern you are studying and the rule that goes with it _____ Pts.				
Able To Do: Recognize words that use the pattern in independent reaching _____ Pts.				
Work Habit Use time wisely _____ Pts.				

SOURCE: Lesson Developed by Sara Frontier, Waterford Village Elementary.

Fourth Grade Reading

Subject: Fourth Grade Reading

Design: Tiered RAFT Plus Lesson

Lesson Component: Learning Target and Student Handout

Understand That (key principles): The characters in stories teach us about life.

Know (facts): Ways that Charlotte and Wilbur were good friends to each other.

Able To Do (skills): Make connections between the story and the world.

Charlotte's Web: RAFT Plus Assignment

Yellow Group

> *Role* = Wilbur

> *Audience* = Charlotte

> *Format* = Skit, song, letter

> *Tasks* = Tell Charlotte three things she taught you about what makes a good friend

Blue Group

> *Role* = Friend who is a good friend

> *Audience* = Another friend who wants to learn how to be a good friend

> *Format* = Skit, letter

> *Tasks* = Share ways to be a good friend based on Charlotte's friendship with Wilbur

Green Group

> *Role* = Mr. President

> *Audience* = Citizens of America

> *Format* = Skit/video, letter, news article

> *Tasks* = Share ways we can become better citizens of the country from what you learned about Charlotte and Wilbur's friendship

Subject: Fourth Grade Reading

Design: Tiered Lessons (done as a tiered RAFT Plus)

Lesson Component: Rubric

Expectations	😊	😐	☹️
Understand that the characters in stories teach us about life			
Know ways that Charlotte and Wilbur were good friends to each other			
Quality Work (As defined by you below)			

Ways I Will Do Quality Work for My Project:

1. _____

2. _____

Fifth Grade Math

Subject: Fifth Grade Math

Design: Tiered Lessons: Task Cards and Technology

Lesson Component: Student Handout

Tiered Lesson Percentages and Decimals

Understand That (key principles): Different ideas or things can be given different names, but may still mean the same idea or thing.

Know (facts):

- Fractions, decimals
- Fractions and decimals represent the same things: numbers that are not whole numbers.

Able To Do (skills):

- Convert fractions and decimals

Tiered Tasks and Technology

Preassessment: Students fill out exit card explaining what they know about fractions and decimals. There are also a few problems for them to attempt:

Write as a fraction: 0.36 _____   0.965 _____

Write as a decimal: 9/100 _____   66/100 _____

Note: This lesson needs to be done in a computer lab or with a classroom set of laptops. Tier 1 and Tier 2 groups will be learning how to convert fractions and decimals by working with the teacher and using a Smart Board to explore sites that teach how to do conversions. Tier 3 students will be teaching themselves or each other. Also note: The BBC sites are British, therefore the pound signs need to be changed to dollar signs before running off the student handouts.

(Continued)

(Continued)

Task Card One

1. Work with your teacher to learn the steps for converting fractions to decimals (using the Web site http://www.mathsisfun.com/converting-fractions-decimals.html).

2. Follow the steps and use your calculator to practice problems on this site (http://www.mathsisfun.com/converting-fractions-decimals.html).

3. When you are ready, get Handout One with the Answer Key and complete it by tomorrow. On the back of the handout, explain how fractions and decimals are the same.

Task Card Two

1. Work with your teacher to learn the steps for converting fractions to decimals (using the Web site http://www.mathsisfun.com/converting-fractions-decimals.html).

2. Go to this site: http://www.bbc.co.uk/skillswise/numbers/fractiondecimalpercentage/comparing/fractionsdecimals/ to practice a few more.

3. When you are ready, do Handout Two. On the back of the handout, explain how fractions and decimals are the same and why it is necessary to have two different "systems."

Task Card Three

1. Go to these sites: http://www.webmath.com/fract2dec.html and http://www.webmath.com/dec2fract.html.

2. Work with a partner to practice converting fractions into decimals and decimals into fractions.

3. When you are ready to work on your own, go to this site and solve problems: http://www.bbc.co.uk/skillswise/numbers/fractiondecimalpercentage/comparing/fractionsdecimals/.

4. Complete Handout Three. On the back of the handout, explain what you've learned about fractions and decimals and discuss how fractions and/or decimals make one thing in our daily life a little easier.

Fractions and Decimals Rubric

Expectations	Great ☺	Good	Okay	Not So Good ☹
Understand: That words have patterns _____ Pts.				
Know: The pattern you are studying and the rule that goes with it _____ Pts.				
Able To Do: Recognize words that use the pattern in independent reaching _____ Pts.				
Work Habit Use time wisely _____ Pts.				

TIERED LESSON: TEACHING TIPS

Lesson Design

- Develop the C U KAN for the lesson prior to designing the tiers. Then you can be sure the tiered lessons you create meet the objectives of the C U KAN.
- *Note to Beginners:* When you first try tiered lessons, it's okay to have just two tiers. You could have most of your students doing one lesson and a small group—either your advanced or struggling learners—working on another tier As you evolve in your skills, you may choose of have more than two tiers.
- Tiered lessons can be short-term or long-term assignments.
- Tiered lessons can be done alone or in groups.
- You can tier classroom discussion questions, homework assignments, or tests. Any lesson can become a tiered lesson.
- Trust us on this one; it seems challenging to tier lessons when you first get started, but as you really begin seeing how your students respond and they are working at their appropriate readiness level, your brain will start to think in tiers. It gets easier!

Management

- Establishing the environment at the beginning of the year will help you manage the class as you begin doing tiered lessons. From day one, begin setting the classroom tone that "Fair is not everybody getting the same thing, fair is everybody getting what they need to be successful." Your class will be prepared and will more readily accept students working at different levels in your classroom.
- Color code your handouts for each tier so you can easily distinguish the tiers.
- Anchor activities are a must when doing tiered lessons. Students will be starting and finishing at different times, so make sure you have a plan for what students must do if they are waiting for you or if they finish early. (See Resources for anchor activity ideas.)
- As you know, advanced learners need more academic challenge. When you allow them to work together from time to time throughout the year, you give them the opportunity to challenge each other and go really deep in their thinking, thus preventing the boredom that can lead to management problems.
- Students with lower readiness levels are often grouped with students who end up doing the work for them. Knowing that someone will always help them out or do the work for them can contribute to the learned helplessness characteristic of these students. When we group lower readiness level students together, oftentimes a new leader emerges. This grouping gives students the support they need and teaches them to grow and build their skills, instead of relying on others.
- While students are working in their tiers, be sure to float around the room giving students the appropriate support they need, at their level, to work with the Understand, Know, and Do of your lesson.

Assessment

- Preassessment is an important part of preparing to do a tiered lesson. You can preassess by giving a short pretest, using journal prompts, exit cards, oral response, etc. (See Resources for more detailed preassessing information.)
- If you are using a rubric, the rubric should have the Understand, Know, Quality Work, and whatever other category you may choose to assess. Even though students are working at different levels of depth and complexity, they should be working toward the same objectives.
- If applicable, have students assess themselves on their projects before you provide the final assessment using the same rubric.

Teacher Self-Assessment

- As you try out tiered lessons, note what's working and what is not. Keep doing what *is* working, and troubleshoot what's not. For example, if you find that students are all finishing at different times or you need to get one tier started and you need something for the other tiers to be working on, you need to plan anchor activities as a management technique.

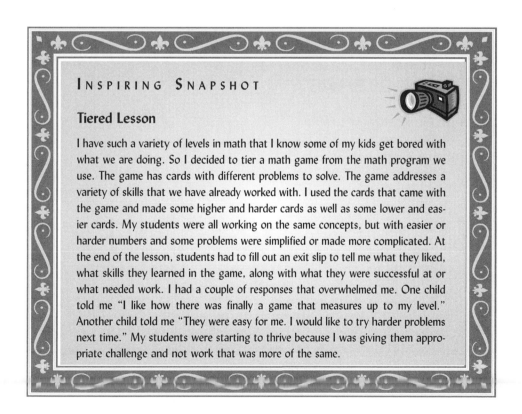

INSPIRING SNAPSHOT

Tiered Lesson

I have such a variety of levels in math that I know some of my kids get bored with what we are doing. So I decided to tier a math game from the math program we use. The game has cards with different problems to solve. The game addresses a variety of skills that we have already worked with. I used the cards that came with the game and made some higher and harder cards as well as some lower and easier cards. My students were all working on the same concepts, but with easier or harder numbers and some problems were simplified or made more complicated. At the end of the lesson, students had to fill out an exit slip to tell me what they liked, what skills they learned in the game, along with what they were successful at or what needed work. I had a couple of responses that overwhelmed me. One child told me "I like how there was finally a game that measures up to my level." Another child told me "They were easy for me. I would like to try harder problems next time." My students were starting to thrive because I was giving them appropriate challenge and not work that was more of the same.

11

Deep-n-Dynamic Design #4

Contracts

TEACHER OVERVIEW

Concept: Commitment

Understand That (key principles):

- Contracts help students see that they are responsible for their own learning.
- Students become self-reflective when we give them ownership of their learning.

Know (facts):

- Teachers can design individual or class contracts.
- Contracts can be designed at different readiness levels.
- Contracts can address behavior as well as academics.

Able To Do (skills):

- Teacher creates either individual or group contracts that have choices and guidelines.
- Students read and commit to the contract by signing it.
- Students are accountable for completing the terms of the contract.

- Students are given a timeline for completing the work on the contracts.

Now You Get It! (Contracts):

- provide challenges and eliminates boredom
- allow for student choice
- develop student commitment and responsibility skills

LITE-N-LEAN WAYS TO USE CONTRACTS

Contracts are a way for teachers to respond to the different learning paces of their students. They are a great way to keep learners engaged when they are finished early or to keep learners on track when they might normally lose track of their progress.

Because a contract is an agreement between two people, it is important to include the teacher's role in the agreement.

Some easy ways to get started are to use simple and generic contracts for students who frequently finish work early, students who have passions to pursue, and even for students who struggle to complete a task.

Anchor Activities Contract

When you finish early, there are many ways you may choose how to use your free time. Keep this list handy as a reference. If you would like to add other early-finishing ideas to your list, please have the idea approved by me.

I, _____, agree to move quickly and quietly to one of the choices listed below. My teacher will allow me to move freely around the room to get the supplies I need as long as I do not disturb other students. If I cannot follow my part of this contract, I will lose my right to choice and free movement and will return to an assignment decided upon by my teacher until otherwise notified.

Student Signature

I, Mrs. Gagnon, agree to allow _____ to move quietly around the room in order to stay engaged in learning activities. I agree to allow for student choice and movement provided other students are not disrupted.

Teacher Signature

Anchor Activities to Choose From:

Read a book or magazine

Continue a story in your writer's notebook

Use mini chalkboards

Practice word wall words (spelling words)

Create magnetic poetry

Use math facts flash cards

Take brain quest quiz

Use math games from shelf

Practice budgeting

Create patterns with pattern blocks

Write problems for partners to solve

Answer the science "question of the week"

Draw vocabulary pictures for our new vocabulary

Create a mini experiment

Write a content song for science or social studies

Self-Selected Study Contract

When you are finished with an assignment early, you may use your free time to pursue an interest of your own!

What would you like to learn more about?

What do you want to know?_____

    ❑ I have a burning question!
    ❑ I really just want to explore and see what I find out.

When will you share information you learn?

    ❑ Informally at class meeting
    ❑ With my teacher in a private conference
    ❑ At the end of the day sharing
    ❑ During a class discussion on this topic
    ❑ Other: _____

Date: _____

What format will you use?

    ❑ Note cards
    ❑ My journal
    ❑ A written report
    ❑ My own book
    ❑ Collage/picture representation
    ❑ Other: _____

I understand that my teacher is allowing me to pursue an interest of my own in my free time. I understand I am responsible for how I act during my free study. If I disrupt class I will no longer be able to pursue this study in class. Also, I will clean up quickly and quietly to rejoin class when the teacher asks.

Student

I agree to allow _____ to work independently on a topic of choice during free time. I agree to provide assistance, guidance, and materials when possible to help this exploration!

Teacher _____

Inch by Inch, It's a Cinch!

This contract is to help you move through today's work easily, allowing you to enjoy more time with anchor activities or with an independent contract.

Student's Role:

- I will follow the directions below, step by step checking off each one as they are done.
- If I get stuck, I will ask two people for help before calling the teacher.
- I will raise my hand to get extra help from the teacher.
- When I am done with the task below, I can move to an activity of my choice!

Student _____

Teacher's Role:

- I will help you step by step through today's task, so that you experience success!
- I will help you see what you *do* know and what you *can* do, so that you see how much you are growing.
- I will check in with you at least three times to make sure you are on the right road.

Teacher _____

Today's Task _____

Steps

- ❑ 1. Put your name on your paper.
- ❑ 2.
- ❑ 3.
- ❑ 4.
- ❑ 5.
- ❑ 6.
- ❑ 7.

DEEP-N-DYNAMIC DESIGNS FOR USING CONTRACTS

K–2 English Language Arts

Subject: K–2 English Language Arts

Design: Contract

Lesson Component: Learning Target and Student Handout

Word Wall Practice

Concept: Patterns

Understand That (key principles):

- Recognizing the patterns of lots of words helps us to read and write easily.
- We all learn word patterns in different ways and at different times.

Know (facts):

- Roles and responsibilities of my contract
- Word wall words

Able To Do (skills):

- Read and write word wall words
- I understand that learning how to spell words helps me become a better reader and writer.
- I understand that we all learn words in different ways and at different times.
- I agree to work during word wall practice on my words to help me become a better reader and writer.
- If I do not work on my word wall practice, I will lose my right to make choices about how I study and will have to practice my words in the way that the teacher tells me.

Student Signature _____

SOURCE: Lesson created by Jessica Pratt.

My Words for the Week
_____ & _____

Must Do: (Monday)

- Write each word in pencil in your writer's notebook.

- Trace the word in crayon.

- Repeat five times.

Choices: (Tuesday, Wednesday, Thursday)

- **Clap** each of your word wall words three times each. Clap over your head for tall letters, at your waist for short letters, and at your knees for letters with a tail.

- **Say** each word in a rhythm, like a song. Say each letter and then say the word again. Ex. C-A-N . . . can, can . . . C-A-N . . . can, can.

- **Type** your words five times on the computer.

- **Scratch** your word's letter by letter onto someone's back. Have them scratch back and guess which word it is.

- Use a different **voice** to say each word. Use a happy voice, a sad voice, a grumpy voice, an angry voice, whispery voice, and a whiny voice.

- Make **matching** cards separated into small chunks.

- Have another **idea**? See me to get the okay!

First Grade Social Studies

Subject: First Grade Social Studies

Design: Contract

Lesson Component: Learning Target and Student Handout

Name_____

School Workers: Everyone Working Together

We are going to explore the different jobs and get to know the many different people that help make our school community so wonderful. You will gather information and have a chance to share your findings with the class. Here are our learning targets:

Concept: Community

Understand That (key principles): A community works best when members have different roles and responsibilities, and work together to function productively.

Know (facts): Roles and responsibilities

Able To Do (skills): Question, summarize

Show what you know about any school worker you choose. Your project must show

- ❑ The person's job
- ❑ How the person needs others to get the job done
- ❑ Why this person is important to our school

My Work Behavior:

— I will stay focused on my work.

— I will try my best.

— I will ask for help if I get stuck.

— I will check in with my teacher to make sure I'm on track.

My Tasks: (check off the task when you have finished)

- ❑ I will select a school worker to interview and set up an interview time with that person.
- ❑ I will review the questions before the interview.
- ❑ I will fill out the interview questions during my interview with the school worker.
- ❑ I will pick a project that is just right for me from the project board.
- ❑ I will share what I learned from my interview in a way that is just right for me.

(Continued)

(Continued)

I understand that my teacher is allowing me to select choices based on my interests and my best way to learn. I understand that I have an important job to do. If I do not do my job on this project, I will lose my right to work at my own pace and will have to join the teacher for help in learning how to stay on task.

Student:_____

Teacher:_____

Interview Questions:

Must Ask:

What is your name? _____

What is the name of your job? _____

What do you do for the school? _____

How do you need other people to do your job?_____

Why is your job important? _____

Your Choice to Ask:

How long have you had this job? _____

What is your favorite thing about your job? _____

What is the hardest thing about your job?_____

How can kids at school help you do your job?_____

SOURCE: Lesson written by Jennifer Hutchinson, Waterford School District.

Name _____

Project Board

Circle the project you will do:

Write a poem about your school worker including all the information you collected during the interview.	Create a play, acting out a school worker's job and all the information you collected during the interview.
Write a thank-you note or card to a school worker. Include information you collected during the interview.	Create a picture or collage about your school worker. Include information you collected during the interview.

Reflection

	Yes ☺	Mostly 😐	Not Really ☹
I picked a just right project all by myself.			
I picked a school worker and interviewed him or her.			
I did a quality job, which means I did my best work.			
I was able to talk about my project and share it with the class and the school worker.			
I included all the MUST ASK information in my project.			
I stayed on task.			

Upper Elementary English Language Arts

Subject: Upper Elementary English Language Arts

Design: Contract

Lesson Component: Learning Target and Student Handout

Book Club Contract

I, _____, will meet the daily, weekly, and unit goals outlined below and on the following page. As my group and I conference weekly with Miss Frontier, we will look over our goals and keep track of our progress. Book club will help me . . . .

Understand That (key principles): Readers can grow and deepen their thinking when they can collaborate and discuss with other readers.

Know (facts): Plot, theme, character, setting of our story

Able To Do (skills):

- Discuss, compare and contrast, summarize, question, conclude
- Develop a plan of action
- Follow through on the plan

Daily Goals:

- ☺ I will complete the assigned reading. I understand that my book club group and I will be setting these reading goals together.
- ☺ I will complete the daily assignments. I understand that these assignments will vary from day to day based on my group's needs and decisions.
- ☺ I will continue to follow the reading behaviors rubric that we created and agreed upon as a class at the beginning of the year. I will do my best to ensure that I am in the "3" range of the rubric during independent reading time.

Weekly Goals:

- ☺ I will meet with my book club group on a weekly basis to discuss our book.
- ☺ I will jot notes on sticky notes during my reading to help me plan for my meetings with my book club group.
- ☺ I will keep up with the reading and assignments.
- ☺ I will make an effort to contribute to each book club conversation and will try to stretch the thinking of the other members in my group.
- ☺ I will honor and respect others' opinions, even if I do not agree with them. If I do disagree with someone, I will do so in a kind and respectful manner.

Unit Goals:

Upon completion of my book, I will choose *one* of the following tasks assigned by my teacher as a final project:

- ☐ Write a book review of the book. Keep in mind that your audience is other students in our class and other interested third graders.
- ☐ Write an alternate ending for the book that you read. Keep in mind that you must include the major characters and your solution must match with the problem presented earlier in the book.
- ☐ Write a song, rap, or poem that is also a retelling of the book. Keep in mind that you *must* include all the story elements in whatever format you choose. A detailed and colorful "album cover" must be included along with your project.
- ☐ The illustration should detail a scene from the book. Think about whether there was one scene that really created some strong mental images for you!
- ☐ (This one you can do with a partner!) Rewrite the story as a play that highlights the important parts of your book. Keep in mind that all of the story elements must be included. Then, perform the play for the class!

Student's Name (printed): _____

Date: _____

Student's Signature: _____

Teacher's Signature: _____

_____

SOURCE: Lesson created by Mary Warner, Waterford, MI.

Upper Elementary Science

Subject: Upper Elementary Science

Design: Whole Class Contract

Lesson Component: C U KAN and Student Handout

Simple Circuits Contract

Concept: Experimentation

Simple Circuit with Light

Understand That (key principles): Scientists use experimentation to make sense of physical phenomena.

Know (facts):

- Vocabulary: electricity, current, series and parallel circuit, variable
- Components of a circuit
- Safety rules for using electricity

Able To Do (skills):

- Design a circuit
- Introduce variables
- Observe impact of change in variables

I, _____, will demonstrate my understanding of the learning objectives by _____ (date).

Working Conditions: (please initial that you understand each condition)

_____ I will work to the best of my abilities.

_____ I will work quietly and independently.

_____ I will problem solve my questions before coming to the teacher.

_____ I will conduct myself in a scientific manner.

_____ I will complete my work in a timely fashion.

Tasks:

Step 1: Decide on two variables that can be changed in a simple circuit.

Step 2: Develop a step by step plan to test each variable.

Step 3: Test each variable.

Step 4 (choose one of the following):

1. Complete a diagram explaining the results of your test.

2. Explain the life application your test could help explain.

3. Write an experiment for fourth graders to test using your variables.

I understand my teacher is giving me freedom to work at a pace that fits my learning style. I agree to have my project ready to share with the class by _____. If I am unable to meet the working conditions, I will return to teacher-directed learning at this point. My teacher will help me with any of the learning tasks that I do not understand or am challenged by.

Teacher Signature _____

Student Signature _____

Date _____

SOURCE: Lesson created by Ken Janczarek and Joseph Martin, Waterford, MI.

LEARNING CONTRACTS: TEACHING TIPS

Lesson Design

- Develop the C U KAN for the lesson prior to designing the contract. This way, you are ensuring the contracts you create meet the objectives of your learning target.
- Contracts should be a blend of skills and content-based activities.
- *Note to Beginners:* When you first try contracts it may be easier to begin with a whole class contract, rather than a contract for a small group or individual. As you evolve your skills, then you can begin doing more complex contracts, like tiered contracts.
- Contracts can be short term or long term.
- As you design your contracts, think about which core activities all students will be expected to complete.
- Also think about what kind of activities can be included in the contracts to support different learning profiles and interests.
- Decide how you will weight each task in the contract. Will you assess everything? Which items best reflect your objectives? Will they all have the same weight or not?

Management

- Allow students to determine the plan for completing their contract by the assigned date. For example, they can determine which activity they want to work on, at what time, or on which day.
- If students do not fulfill their contract obligations, have them sign a Student Responsibility form. (See Resources for an example of this form.) Students can also help you determine what the consequences should be for not completing their contract.
- Be sure to have an anchor activity for students to work on if they finish early.
- When students complete their contracts, have them paperclip completed assignments together with the contract on top. Have a basket for each class period's work.
- Expect and encourage students to help each other, before coming to you for help. ("See three, then see me.")
- Create three-sided table tents labeled, "Hard at Work," "HELP!" and "Finished." (Be sure to check the finished work to see if it is quality work before allowing students to move to anchor activities.) While students are working on their contracts, be sure to float around the room and check to see that they are on task.
- Begin the class by checking in with students to make a management plan for the day's work session. Make a plan for the students who need to leave the class and managing/sharing materials.

Assessment

- Exit cards are a great tool for students' self-assessment while working on contracts.

- If you have several activities on a contract, you can tell students you will be assessing them on having all the assignments completed, and that you will grade one assignment of their choice and one that you will select randomly.
- You could give a traditional quiz or test at the end of the lesson or unit.

Teacher Self-Assessment

- As you try out contracts, note what's working and what is not. Keep doing what *is* working, and troubleshoot what's not. For example, if some students are not living up to their contracts, have them sign a Student Responsibility Form.

INSPIRING SNAPSHOT

Contracts

DJ was in my kindergarten class last year. As a young boy full of life, curiosity, and mischief, he was often unfocused on the work at hand. I had recently began using work contracts with my five- and six-year-olds as a way to help them focus on what has been completed, what they want to do next, and a general tool for organization and helping them make choices. Since my students are young and just developing literacy skills, the contracts are in the form of a pie graph with various centers and learning activities represented with a picture. Students circle the picture of what they intend to accomplish during the week (setting goals) and as they complete the center or activity, they color in that part of the pie graph.

I thought DJ had been doing well with the contracts. He seemed more focused since we began them but I had no idea of the influence the use of contracts had on this young learner.

One afternoon I received a phone call from DJ's mom explaining there was a sickness in the family and he would be out of school for four days. She informed me, "DJ did not jump up and yell with excitement about missing school. His *first* question/concern was, "Mom, what will I do about my commitment to my contract work?" What a testimony to the power that had been created by establishing individual responsibility, choice, and commitment!

12

Deep-n-Dynamic Design #5

Stations

TEACHER OVERVIEW

Concept: Varying Learning Profiles

Understand That (key principles):

- Stations provide interest and challenge for all types of learners.

Know (facts):

- Stations are areas set up around a classroom. Students rotate to different stations to explore new topics or practice skills.
- Stations can be designed based on input (chunk), process (chew), or products (check).
- Stations can be differentiated by readiness level. You can design stations so that high ability learners have opportunities to broaden their knowledge and go deeper into a topic. Stations can also be adapted to provide remedial work for struggling learners.
- Stations can be developed around different learning styles or intelligences, or they can be interest-based stations.

- Structured stations are stations where students learn objectives through specific tasks. Management rules are set and workspace is provided. Structured stations allow learners to work on specific applications of a lesson or unit and to independently practice a skill.
- Exploratory stations are stations where students explore ideas and objectives through discovery, creating, solving problems, inventing, manipulating at their own pace, and understanding.

Able To Do (skills):

- Students may rotate to each station and try each activity or students may be assigned to specific stations developed to meet specific needs.
- Depending on the complexity of the stations, the teacher may need to do some preteaching before the students go to the stations.
- Station tasks should be active and engaging for all types of learners.
- The teacher needs to move about from station to station to monitor the students and make adjustments if needed.
- Students may reflect on what they learned in the stations through logs, self-assessments, or short quizzes.

Now You Get It!
Stations

- are fun, active, and engaging ways to learn information
- help students be more independent in their learning
- are a great way to incorporate technology

LITE-N-LEAN WAYS TO USE STATIONS

Lite-n-lean stations will be set up for only a short period of time in your classroom. A lite–n-lean station where students rotate through in an hour allows us to offer various ways of *chunking* and *chewing* information. Whenever we can break the content into segments (for example, three branches of government, animal and plant kingdoms, stages in a life cycle, etc.), we can set up *chunk* stations where each station focuses on one part of the content. Whenever we can develop varying tasks that will allow students to process learning in their unique way, we can set up those tasks as *chew* stations.

Lite-n-Lean Chunk (input) Stations:

- Each station has different content for students to take in.
- Each station presents content in different ways—charts and graphs, readings, video, exploring on the computer, exploring with a partner, etc.

Lite-n-Lean Chew (process) Stations:

- Each station focuses on processing learning through one multiple intelligence (music, art, body, etc.) or learning style (visual, auditory, kinesthetic).
- Each station focuses on processing learning using of the Vital Know-Hows. Using the same content or learning target, have students use discussion, reflection, research, writing, etc. to explore their understandings.

Examples: Lite-n-Lean Stations

Life Cycle of Butterflies (Chunk Stations)

Kindergarten. Students visit stations to learn about the life cycle of the butterfly. In one station, they watch a video or go to the Web site http:// www.museum.vic.gov.au/bioinformatics/butter/images/kerslive2.htm to learn about the butterfly life cycle. In another, they read a book about the life cycle of a butterfly. In the third station, they look at photographs of butterflies at varying stages of the life cycle.

Contractions (Chew Stations)

Third Grade. Give the following prompt to students, followed by the instructions below for each station: "You'll visit each of the three centers and you shouldn't waste a moment! When you are finished with your stations, you can move directly to your anchor activity. Contractions: they're everywhere, aren't they?"

- *Station 1*: Memory Matching Game. With a partner, match the contractions and the word used to make the contraction (e.g., *wouldn't – would not*).
- *Station 2*: Complete the computer quiz that is found on the Web site we used to gather our information about contractions: http:// www.manatee.k12.fl.us/sites/elementary/palmasola/con12a.htm.
- *Station 3*: Create a reference chart of contractions and words contracted based on the list we brainstormed in class. Add three more of your own.

Time (Chew Stations)

Second Grade. Give the following prompt to students, following by the instructions below for each station: "We will rotate among three stations every fifteen minutes. Clock on!"

- *Station 1*: Write out a schedule of your day using hours and minutes.
- *Station 2*: Create a list of what you can do in one minute, two minutes, and three minutes. (Hop, sit quietly, hum a tune, etc.) Practice your timing with a partner.
- *Station 3*: Convert the times from hours and minutes to just minutes.

DEEP-N-DYNAMIC DESIGNS
FOR USING STATIONS

First–Second Grade Math

Subject: First–Second Grade Math

Design: Stations

Lesson Component: Learning Target

Money

Concept: Value

Understand That (key principles): Societies create money as a measure of the value of goods and services.

Know (facts):

- Penny, dime, nickel, quarter, dollar, etc.
- The value for each coin
- The symbols $ and C
- Terms: value, worth

Able To Do (skills):

- Match a written value with sets of equivalent coins.
- Tell the amount of money in cents up to a dollar, in dollars up to $100.

Now You Get It!

Students rotate between three stations. At the end of each station, students will self-assess using an exit card that they place into labeled folders so the teacher can check on their progress.

Subject: First–Second Grade Math

Design: Stations

Lesson Component: Planning Guide

Station 1: Money History

Objectives Met: Understanding how societies use money

Materials:

- Sheet with money facts or the book *Round and Round the Money Goes: What Money Is and How We Use It* by Melvin Berger. (Tape or plan to have someone read the book.)
- Colored pencils and paper

Station 2: Coin Stack

Objectives Met: Knowing value of coins

Materials:

- Five cards with values written on them: 73, $1.15, 40, $12.50, $52.00
- Manipulatives: Coins and bills

Station 3: Price It!

Objectives Met: Knowing symbols, saying amounts of money, recognizing value of goods

Materials:

- Six envelopes with values written on the front
- Weekly newspaper sales inserts
- Scissors

Subject: First–Second Grade Math

Design: Stations

Lesson Component: Student Handouts

Station 1: Money History

- Read about the history of money and about the history of the different coins.
- Either draw a picture or write a story that shows people exchanging money for goods or services.

Station 2: Add It Up!

- There are five cards before you with an amount of money written on them.
- Work with play coins and bills to create a stack or pile on top of each card that matches the value of that card. Work with a partner to check your work.
- If you finish, choose one card and come up with two other ways of reaching the same value.

Station 3: Price It

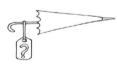

- There are six envelopes with values written on the front. Working with a partner, each of you should choose three envelopes.
- Take turns reading the values of your envelopes.
- Look through the weekly sales flier and find an item that matches each value. Say to your partner, for example, "The pencils on page 2 are $1.99."
- Cut out the picture and put it in that envelope. Continue until each envelope has one item in it.

Subject: First-Second Grade Math

Design: Stations

Lesson Component: Student Handouts

Money Station Exit Card: Self-Assessment

Station # _____

NAME:_____

1. I did a good job. _____ _____

2. I got it! _____ _____

3. I finished my work. _____ _____

This is what I learned:

K–2 Reading

Subject: K–2 Reading

Design: Stations

Lesson Component: Learning Target and Planning Guide

Segmenting Words

Concept: Patterns

Understand That (key principles): Language has patterns and when we recognize the patterns we can use the language effectively.

Know (facts):

- Beginning, middle, end sounds
- Rules for dominos and memory games

Able To Do (skills):

- Segment words into parts
- Use a graphic organizer (Column number chart)
- Work in groups for a goal or to play a game
- Move quickly and quietly between stations

Now You Get It!

After rotating through the stations, students read a story using the key vocabulary words. The teacher asks students to share as a group what they are learning about word patterns and how that is helping them learn to read. Teacher makes a chart with each student's name and records who is able to identify beginning, middle, and end sounds and makes note of who needs additional work in this area.

Materials:

- Station 1—Break the Code: five cups, thirty keys, picture cards
- Station 2—Sound Domino: rhyme pictures glued on craft sticks
- Station 3—Column number sheet (2, 3, 4, 5), various objects with two to five letter sounds discernable
- Timer to alert children to change stations

Station 1: Key to the Code

Objectives Met: Beginning, middle, and end sounds, segmenting word parts

- Divide into pairs of two.
- Each pair takes one cup of ten keys and one pile of picture cards.
- One student in each pair speaks in "secret code." This student segments words for his or her partner. The "secret code" student turns over one card at a time and says the name of the word in "code." For example, if the picture is of a ham, the student says /h/ /a/ /m/.

(Continued)

(Continued)

> - The "code breaker" is to break the code by telling his or her partner the name of the picture without seeing the picture. If the code is /h/ /a/ /m/, the code breaker's correct response would be "ham." If the correct response is given, the "code breaker" takes a key from the cup.
> - The "secret code" student continues to give picture names in code and the code breaker continues to break the code until all ten keys are gone or until time is called.

Station 2: Sound Dominos

Objectives Met: Beginning, middle, and end sounds, working cooperatively

- Divide into groups of two-three students.
- Each student chooses four dominos and places the rest face down in a pile.
- The object of the game is to get rid of your dominos by matching picture sounds (beginning, middle, or end).
- One player from each group places a domino on the tabletop or floor.
- The other player then matches one picture on that domino with one of his or her own (for example, cat and car pictures match because they both begin with /c/). If a player has no match, that player must choose from the pile until one is found.
- Partners take turns adding dominos to the pattern. A player wins when he or she runs out of dominos. If all dominos are used, the player with the fewest unmatched dominos wins.

Station 3: Classifying Objects

Objectives Met: Organize information into a graph, vocabulary

- Take a small bag of objects and a number graph.
- Pull an object from the bag and count the number of phonemes you hear in the object's name.
- Place the object under the correct column on the number graph. For example, a key would be placed under the 2 column; a penny would be placed under the 4 column.
- Continue until your bag is empty.

SOURCE: Designed by Erin Davis and Amy Childs.

Grades 2–5 Vocabulary

Subject: Grades 2–5 Vocabulary

Design: Stations

Lesson Component: Student Handout

Concept: Learning Styles

Understand That (key principles): We all learn in different ways; therefore, we need to find ways of studying that work for our learning style.

Know (facts):
- Vocabulary words for this lesson

Able To Do (skills):
- Move quickly and quietly between stations
- Reflect on what works for you as a learner

Now You Get It:
After completing the stations, students reflect on which station best helped them learn the words.

Vocabulary

Vocabulary Station # 1: Matching Brain Games
    Your Choice:

1. Make vocabulary flash cards by putting the word on half the card and the definition in your own words on the other card. If you finish, trade cards and play the game with each other's cards.

2. Make a concentration matching game. Put the words on one card and the definitions on another card. Here's how to play…
   a. Shuffle the cards and lay them face down in a square on the table.
   b. At each turn, the player turns over two cards (one at a time) and keeps them if they match numbers. A successful match means the player gets to take another turn.
   c. When a player turns over two cards that do not match numbers, those cards are turned face down again and it becomes the next player's turn.
   d. The player with the most cards wins!

(Continued)

(Continued)

Vocabulary Station # 2: Write It/Draw It!
   Your Choice:

1. Draw a picture to show your understanding of the vocabulary words.

2. Write a story using your vocabulary words.

3. Write a story for children using words and pictures.

(If you don't finish this during station time, please take it home to finish.)

Vocabulary Station # 3: Say That Definition!

1. Two people need to become the card reader and the scorekeeper. While the score keeper is setting up a scoring board, the card reader will divide the rest of the group into two teams by numbering them 1, 2, 1, 2, etc. The 1s go on one side of the tables, the 2s go on the other side.

2. Decide which team goes first.

3. The card reader draws a word from the pile and reads the word. The first person on the team that goes first needs to give the definition. (The other team members are not allowed to help.)

4. If the person gets the definition correct, that team gets the point. If not, the first person on the other team gets a chance at the word.

5. Continue taking turns this way until station time is called. The team that has the most points at that time wins the game.

Vocabulary Stations Exit Card: Self-Assessment

NAME: _____

		LOW		HIGH	
1. I used my station time wisely.	1	2	3	4	5
2. I completed the station tasks.	1	2	3	4	5

Which station do you feel helped you understand the vocabulary words the best? Explain why.

How can knowing this help you study better at home?

Third Grade Science

Subject: Third Grade Science

Design: Stations

Lesson Component: Learning Target and Planning Guide

Plants

Concept: Cycles

Understand That (facts): All living things go through a cycle with a beginning, middle, and end.

Know (facts):

- Vocabulary: Cycle, roots, stem, leaves, seedling, germination, pollination
- The stages of plant life cycles

Able To Do (skills):

- Sequence
- Record observations
- Compare and contrast
- Discuss

Now You Get It!

Students will rotate between three stations for fifteen minutes per station. Each student will then create and label a picture that shows the life cycle of a plant.

Materials:

Plant Research	Act It Out!	Look and Compare
• Books on plant life cycle • Question sheet with ten questions on it (four–five copies, so everyone can have their own) • Books on tape about plant life cycle • TV/DVD with United Streaming video	• Envelope with slips of paper identifying seed, germination, sunlight and water, roots and stems, flowers, germination	• Three live plants (all at different stages and each with a different color on it), and one dead plant (with a color on it) • Seeds (with a color attached to it) • Cycle card sheet • Crayons

Subject: Third Grade Science

Design: Stations

Lesson Component: Student Handouts

Station 1: Plant Research

Use the books available to look up answers to questions. As a team, divide the questions among you. You must each choose a question from the A column, B column, and C column. Share your answers with each other when you are done.

Station 2: Act It Out!

In the envelope provided, pull out a slip of paper with a part of the plant (roots, seedling, leaves, etc.) or an action that occurs (germination, pollination, sunlight, etc.) during the life cycle of a plant. Act out the part or action and have the others guess what you are. After all parts have been identified, form a circle with each part/action in the order of the life cycle.

Station 3: Look and Compare

Live plants have been color coded for sequential identification purposes. Use the Cycle Card and use appropriate crayons to color in the order of a plant's life cycle. (The cycle card is a card with four blank lines. Students must color code with a crayon the correct stage of the plant from beginning to end.)

LEARNING STATIONS: TEACHING TIPS

Lesson Design

- Develop the C U KAN for the lesson prior to designing the stations. This way you can be sure the stations you create meet the objectives of the C U KAN.
- *Note to Beginners:* When you first try stations, it's easier to begin with fewer, less complex stations. As your skills evolve, then you can begin doing more complex stations, tiered stations, etc.
- You may create different stations that each meet a different C U KAN objective. You could combine structured stations with exploratory stations.
- Stations can be short term (a day of vocabulary stations) or long term.
- Stations can be tiered. Students can be grouped by readiness levels and then rotate through the stations. If you color code the groups (Red, Blue, Green) you can match the handouts at the station to the color/readiness level of the group.
- It's impossible to make sure that all stations take the same amount of time. Be sure to have an anchor activity for students to work on if they finish early in the stations.

Management

- Use an overhead timer or Time Timer so that students can keep track of how much time they have in the station. Use chimes, a gong, a whistle, etc. to let the groups know that it's time to rotate the station.
- Again, be sure to have an anchor activity for students to work on if they finish early.
- Appoint a station leader who makes sure that the station is reorganized before moving on to the next station.
- Expect and encourage students to help each other, before coming to you for help. ("See three, then see me.")
- While students are working at their stations, be sure to float around the room and check to see that they are on task.

Assessment

- Students should be clear about the Understand, Know, and Able To Do that they are learning at the station.
- Exit cards are a great tool for having students self-assess in stations. (See examples in this section.)
- You can have reflection sheets or worksheets at stations that can be graded.
- You could give a traditional quiz or test about what they learned in the stations.

Teacher Self-Assessment

As you try out stations, note what's working and what is not. Keep doing what *is* working, and troubleshoot what's not. (For example, if some students are not able to handle being in stations, have a plan for pulling them out and giving them an alternative assignment to work on that day.)

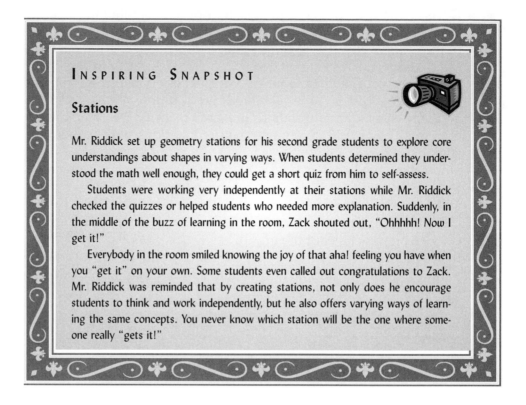

INSPIRING SNAPSHOT

Stations

Mr. Riddick set up geometry stations for his second grade students to explore core understandings about shapes in varying ways. When students determined they understood the math well enough, they could get a short quiz from him to self-assess.

Students were working very independently at their stations while Mr. Riddick checked the quizzes or helped students who needed more explanation. Suddenly, in the middle of the buzz of learning in the room, Zack shouted out, "Ohhhhh! Now I get it!"

Everybody in the room smiled knowing the joy of that aha! feeling you have when you "get it" on your own. Some students even called out congratulations to Zack. Mr. Riddick was reminded that by creating stations, not only does he encourage students to think and work independently, but he also offers varying ways of learning the same concepts. You never know which station will be the one where someone really "gets it!"

13

Deep-n-Dynamic Design #6

Compacting

TEACHER OVERVIEW

Concept: Challenge

Understand That (key principles):

- Advanced learners need to experience academic challenge.
- Advanced learners need to learn to take risks and persevere on tasks.

Know (facts):

- Compacting is a strategy that differentiates for high ability students.
- Compacting involves three basic steps:
  1. The teacher assesses what students already know about the material to be studied.
  2. A plan is made for students to skip what they already know and to learn what is not known.
  3. A plan is made for students to use the available time to accelerate their study or enrich their learning.

Able To Do (skills):

- Students are given a pretest to determine what they already know about the unit to be studied.

- Students who score 85–90 percent or above on the pretest are expected to complete an alternative study or project.
- Students who test out are accountable for learning materials they did not know on the pretest.
- Students are expected to sign a contract with expectations for task accomplishment during class time. Students also complete a daily work log.
- Students may share their projects or research with the rest of the class.
- Students who compact may choose to work on group projects.

Now You Get It!
Compacted lessons:

- allow high ability students to move more quickly through the curriculum
- provide challenges and eliminate boredom
- are a simple and organized format for teachers to accelerate advanced students

LITE-N-LEAN WAYS TO COMPACT

Getting started with compacting can be as simple as noticing which students have more readiness or have acquired skills quickly. These students need more challenge! Try one of the following during a day's lesson to keep them moving forward. If students get off track with their challenge, simply ask them to rejoin the rest of the class.

Ways to Provide Challenge
Have students begin an assignment with the most difficult problems first. Having students do fewer but more difficult problems reduces unneeded repetition and engages them at the appropriate readiness level.
Advanced students can do enrichment activities found in the textbook or in supplements to the textbook.
Allow these students to opt out of a day's lesson and self-select how to use their time. (Independent project, finish other work, computer time)

DEEP-N-DYNAMIC DESIGNS FOR COMPACTING

Lower Elementary Social Studies

Subject: Lower Elementary Social Studies

Design: Compacting

Lesson Component: C U KAN and Student Handout

Communities, Citizens, and Change Over Time: Alternative Projects

You have demonstrated in your Quick Write that you already know the essential learning related to citizens living together in a community. You will get to demonstrate deeper understanding by selecting a mini-project to work on for the next two weeks. You will share what you learn with your classroom community. You will be graded on quality, accuracy, and creativity. You will still be expected to take part in whole class mini-lessons each day.

Concept: Interrelationships

Understand That (key principles): Citizens give to their communities and depend on others in their communities.

Know (facts):

- ways that people can get along with each other
- ways that people depend on each other
- ways that people give to one another

Able To Do (skills):

- self-select a project
- work on it to completion

Select a mini project to demonstrate your learning:

- **Picture Book**
  Choose a community (your home, school, neighborhood, parent's work place) and create a picture book that includes pictures of at least five different community members, how they give to the community, how the community depends on them, and how they depend on the community.

- **Community Model**
  Choose a community (your home, school, neighborhood, parent's work place) and build a model, using any materials you choose, that includes at least five different community members, how they give to the community, how the community depends on them, and how they depend on the community. Using any material you choose, create a model of our community.

(Continued)

(Continued)

- **Two Communities Report**
  Choose two communities (two homes, schools, neighbor-hoods, work places) and write a story or report that includes at least five different community members, how they give to the community, how the community depends on them, and how they depend on the community.

- **Bulletin Board**
  Choose a community (your home, school, neighborhood, parent's work place) and create a bulletin board in the hallway or classroom that includes at least five different community members, how they give to the community, how the community depends on them, and how they depend on the community.

- **Role Play**
  Take on the role of a community member who lives in your town. Present to the class a play about this person's life. Be sure to include how this citizen gives to the com-munity, how the community depends on them, and how they depend on the community. They should interact with at least four other community members.

SOURCE: Adapted from lesson created by Jennifer Hutchinson, Waterford, MI.

Lower Elementary Math

Subject: Lower Elementary Math

Design: Compacting

Lesson Component: Student Handout

My Learning Contract
Creating and Solving Daily Story Problems

Congratulations! You are a computation expert! Because of your hard work I would like to give you a chance to challenge yourself and the rest of the class by becoming the second grade coteacher with me!

Understand That (key principles): Story problems show us how to use math in real life ways.

Know (facts): Clue words that guide us to an efficient way to solve the problem (more than, less than, divided among, etc.)

Able To Do (skills): Write story problems; discuss quality of story problems with peers or the teacher.

Working Conditions:

- I will be eager to work during math each and every day.
- I will not bother anyone or call attention to the fact that I am doing different work than others.

Learning Skills:

- I will include the math skill that the rest of the class is working on (money, time, etc.) in the story problems I create.
- I will discuss my problems with a partner (or the teacher) to make sure they are clear and meaningful to the real world before sharing with the class.

For My Independent Project:

- I will show my story problems to the teacher weekly. If they are accurate, my story problems may be used for the class to solve in the weeks to come.
- At the end of the marking period, I will trade a collection of my story problems with another student to solve each other's problems.

By signing my name on the line, I agree to the above learning contract. If I do not follow my contract I will have to go back to solving the teacher-made daily story problems.

Student's Signature. _____ Date. _____

Teacher's Signature: _____ Date: _____

Subject: Lower Elementary Math
Design: Compacting
Lesson Component: Rubric

Story Problem Journal Reflection

Name_____

	Good	**Alright**	**Try Again**
Understand: Story problems show us how to use math in real life ways.	*Creates new story problem scenarios with real life applications.*	*Restates already existing problems in own words*	*Unable to create story problems that are solvable.*
Know: Words that tell what kind of math to do.	*Creatively uses key math words*	*Uses key math words*	*Does not use key math words or uses incorrect word*
Skill: Discusses story problems with peers/teacher	*Creatively shares story problems with class*	*Shares story problems when asked*	*Does not share with others*

Reflection

- Looking back at your story problems, where did you do the best? Why do you say that? _____

- What was most difficult for you? What helped you improve or overcome your problems? _____

_____

SOURCE: Lesson created by Abbie Schires, Waterford, MI.

Upper Elementary Science

Subject: Upper Elementary Science

Design: Compacted Contract

Lesson Component: C U KAN and Student Handout

Simple Machines

I, _____, will demonstrate my understanding of the learning objectives by _____ (date).

Understand That (key principles): Humans construct knowledge in many ways.

Know (facts): The way humans attempt to construct meaning sometimes leads to misconceptions.

Able To Do (skills): Clearly explain or demonstrate a misconception.

Working Conditions

- ❑ I will work independently to reach my goal without drawing attention to myself.
- ❑ I will work in a scientific manner.
- ❑ I will problem solve my questions before taking them to the teacher.
- ❑ I will complete my work in a timely fashion.

Tasks

- Step 1: Choose one simple machine misconception below and explain the misconception.
  - ○ Machines put in more work than people put out.
  - ○ A screw is its own category of simple machine.
  - ○ The number of pulleys decreases the amount of work done.
- Step 2: Choose one of the following. Make sure your work shows your understanding and knowledge of the concepts listed above.
  1. Make a poster that represents the misconception and the problems that would result if people still believe the misconception.
  2. Complete a scientific investigation form that explains your misconception. Explain the problems that would result if people still believe the misconception.
  3. Create a skit to represent your misconception and the problems that would result if people still believe the misconception.

Because you have demonstrated that you already have basic knowledge about simple machines, I am giving you the freedom to work independently on a project of your choice. I am looking forward to you sharing your results with the class.

Teacher Signature

Student Signature_____

Date _____

SOURCE: Lesson created by Ken Janczarek and Joseph Martin, Waterford, MI.

Any Grade/Subject

Subject: Any

Design: Compacted Contract

Lesson Component: C U KAN and Student Handout

Student Contract
For Advanced Learning Opportunities

Concept: Challenge

Understand That (key principles): Lifelong learners grow from taking on appropriately challenging learning experiences.

Know (facts):

- perseverance
- risk-taking

Able To Do (skills):

- self-select a project
- work on it to completion

STUDENT NAME: _____

I have tested out of some of my classwork and will be able to use that time to complete other tasks at my own pace.

Student: I agree to the following:

I will select and complete an alternative assignment that is challenging for me.

I will use my time wisely each day and record my daily efforts in my "Log of Project Work."

I will set up conference times with my teacher to review my work.

I will be respectful of others and not brag about my work.

I will complete the projects I choose to do and turn them in to the teacher.

Student Signature _____Date _____

Teacher: I agree to help this student follow this plan by providing guidance, questioning, feedback, and materials (based on availability).

Teacher Signature _____Date _____

COMPACTING: TEACHING TIPS

Lesson Design

- Compacting is used for students who can pass a pretest to show that they already know the C U KAN for the unit. Activities should then be designed to deepen the students' knowledge within the C U KAN objectives.
- *Note to Beginners:* When you first try compacting, you may want to offer fewer options for what students can do with the time they have bought. As you evolve your skills, then you can begin offering more choices and/or letting the students design the choices.
- As you plan the compacted activities, think about ways to support different learning profiles and interests.
- Some compacted lesson designs engage advanced learners through choice menus, orbital studies (independent, long-term studies), or student-designed projects.

Management

- Students who compact out of the unit must sign a contract regarding their obligations for working independently. If students do not fulfill their contract obligations, they are brought back with the rest of the class.
- Students might also contract for the grade they are going to work for on their project.
- Students need to keep a daily log of work accomplished and report to you daily by exit card or brief conference. There must be a method of accountability in place for these students.
- If students are going to be working away from your classroom, be sure that other adults are aware of where the students are supposed to be.

Assessment

- Exit cards are a great self-assessment tool for students' work on compacted assignments.
- The pretest grade can be averaged with the grade they earned on their project.
- You can require students to take any quizzes or final tests that the rest of the class is taking. Students will be expected to prepare for the test on their own time.

Teacher Self-Assessment

As you try out compacting, reflect on what's working and what is not working. For example, if you have too many students testing out of a unit, you may need to rethink your pre-assessment. Generally, only around the top 3 percent of your class should be able to pass a pretest.

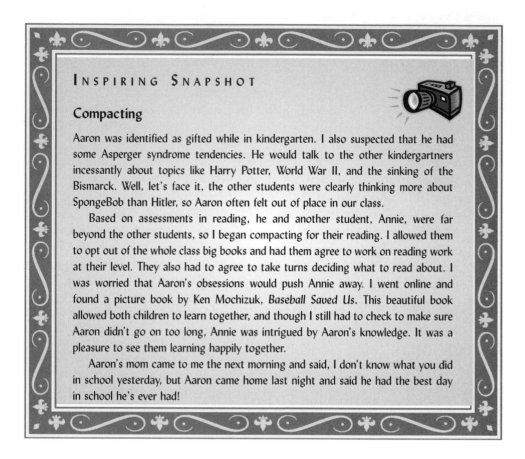

INSPIRING SNAPSHOT

Compacting

Aaron was identified as gifted while in kindergarten. I also suspected that he had some Asperger syndrome tendencies. He would talk to the other kindergartners incessantly about topics like Harry Potter, World War II, and the sinking of the Bismarck. Well, let's face it, the other students were clearly thinking more about SpongeBob than Hitler, so Aaron often felt out of place in our class.

Based on assessments in reading, he and another student, Annie, were far beyond the other students, so I began compacting for their reading. I allowed them to opt out of the whole class big books and had them agree to work on reading work at their level. They also had to agree to take turns deciding what to read about. I was worried that Aaron's obsessions would push Annie away. I went online and found a picture book by Ken Mochizuk, *Baseball Saved Us*. This beautiful book allowed both children to learn together, and though I still had to check to make sure Aaron didn't go on too long, Annie was intrigued by Aaron's knowledge. It was a pleasure to see them learning happily together.

Aaron's mom came to me the next morning and said, I don't know what you did in school yesterday, but Aaron came home last night and said he had the best day in school he's ever had!

14

Assessment and Grading in the Inspiring Classroom

Those who have most at stake in the old culture, or are most rigid in their beliefs, try to summon people back to the old ideas.

—Marilyn Ferguson

Before planting the first seed, a skilled gardener draws up a gardening plan. He determines the soil conditions, amount of sunlight and shade at each time of day, and checks to make sure his tools are in good condition. During the growing season, he knows there is ongoing work to be done. Changing weather conditions and the occasional garden pests require the gardener to continually monitor his garden's progress. He assesses the growth of his plants and uses the information to make decisions to keep the plants healthy and strong.

Like gardeners, teachers need to create a clear plan for learning, continually assessing students' growth and understanding, and making thoughtful decisions that lead students to reach learning goals.

Let's listen to Ms. Johnson, a third grade teacher in an Inspiring Classroom, and see how she uses assessment before, during, and after learning to monitor the progress of her students toward reaching the learning target (plan):

> Okay class, we'll be starting the new unit on the environment. Before we get started, I'd like to see what you already know, so I'm going to have you do a quick write on a half sheet of paper. For the last seven minutes before lunch, I would like you to write whatever you think you know about the pollution problems in our environment, types of pollution, and what people are or should be doing to help the environment. You can add diagrams and drawings if you like. You will turn this exit card in to me as you leave for lunch.

A few days later:

> I have gone over your quick write exit cards, and I noticed that you all have a pretty good background and understanding about issues concerning the environment. So, I figured this would be a great time to offer you some choices in our unit about what you study and how you present what you learn. Here are the target objectives for the unit.

Ms. Johnson posts the C U KAN objectives on chart paper:

Understand

- All living things are dependent upon the environment to sustain life.

Know

- Reuse, reduce, recycle (ways humans help)
- Types of pollution

Able To Do

- Summarize information from your notes

Now You Get It!

- Using the notes you have gathered, select from a choice menu a way to share what you Know and Understand about your group's type of pollution.

Ms. Johnson continues:

> Let's go over them together because you will need to include the Understand and Know learning targets in whatever project you decide to do.

During the discussion, students brainstorm, and Ms. Johnson notes questions and misconceptions the students have about the learning targets:

> Your Able To Do skill for this unit is note-taking. Note-taking is one of the vital know-hows that lifelong learners need, so I will be showing you how to take notes as you research in preparation for your final project. Remember that you will get points for turning in quality notes.

Ms. Johnson models the process and scaffolds the instruction of note-taking as students gather data from various sources. She "kid watches" over the next few days, observing how students are progressing at taking notes and gathering data for their projects. She wraps up the lesson as follows:

> Now, class, you have spent the last few days taking notes and becoming experts on the area of pollution you have chosen to study. Remember that your project needs to meet the objectives for this unit. I would like you to look over your notes and, for five minutes, discuss with your learning partner how well you understand and know the learning targets for this unit. After five minutes, I'll ask for a "thumbs up" on how you are doing.

After five minutes, students give a thumbs up if they've got it, a sideways thumb if they have some but not all of the information, and a thumbs down if they are not getting it. From this information, Ms. Johnson determines who needs more help, who might be willing to help others, and who's doing fine.

On the final day of the project, Ms. Johnson again discusses assessment:

> It's time for the Now You Get It! part of the project. Today you will be presenting or turning in your final project for the environmental unit. Take out the rubric you received a few days ago. Recall that you are being graded on how well you present the Understand and Know objectives in your project, the quality of your project, and your notes. Now it's time for you to reflect on how well you think you have met these objectives. As you self-assess using the rubric, you should be thinking, "How do I think I did? How do I think that compares to Ms. Johnson's opinion?" You also need to reflect on what you feel you did that was quality work and what you would do better next time. I will then assess and grade your project using the same rubric. Since I am the final evaluator for this project, it will be my grade that goes in the grade book. I am excited to see your final results.

As you can see, Ms. Johnson created her lesson with the end in mind, so she was able to plan engaging and meaningful ways to help her students succeed in meeting those objectives. She preassessed her students to see where their skills and knowledge were strong and where they were lacking. During learning, she used the preassessment information to help her effectively *chunk, chew,* and *check* her lesson. She continued to assess and provide feedback to both the whole class and individual students during the learning process. The students were expected to reflect upon and internalize what they needed to do to grow their skills. The students did a final self-reflection using the rubric that the teacher also used as a final assessment. This ongoing assessment is an essential component of the inspiring classroom.

It is important to note that assessment and grading *are not the same.* Assessment occurs throughout learning. It is an ongoing process for collecting data about students in order to make sound instructional decisions. Assessment occurs in many forms and includes students self-reflecting about their own learning. Grading, on the other hand, occurs at the end of learning. It is how we communicate our final judgment about how successful each student has been at hitting the learning target. Grading and assessment are made easy when we use the C U KAN framework to define our learning target clearly. The C U KAN framework also makes it easy for us to provide ongoing feedback to students and for students to self-assess during learning.

ONGOING ASSESSMENT

Assessment in the Inspiring Classroom is the continuous process of gathering data about our students before, during, and after learning. This ongoing assessment keeps us, and our students, informed of progress, which allows for more efficient and effective use of our instructional time. When we are informed, we no longer have to make a best guess about our students' needs or hope that the class understands our lesson. We *know* what our students need, and we *know* whether they are on target or not. Listed below are ideas for assessing before, during, and after learning.

Assessment Before Learning

Once we have established the learning objectives (C U KAN) for our unit, we can honor our students by determining their interests, attitudes, and learning styles as well as by preassessing to find out what they already know. (See Figure 14.1.) Assessment before learning is essential prior to beginning a unit of study where we know our students will already have a great span of previous knowledge or existing skills. Preassessment buys us more instructional time by limiting repetitive instruction. It provides the data that help us design the most efficient learning path for our class.

Ms. Johnson's preassessment gave her the information she needed to design efficient instruction. By realizing that her students had a strong handle on the content, she decided this unit would be a great time to focus on instructing the skill of note-taking. It would have been a waste of Ms. Johnson's time to directly instruct the whole class on terms and concepts. By preassessing, we gather the data we need to write a lesson that is efficient use of our instructional time. Even if we save one day of instructional time, over time, we could be buying ourselves weeks of instructional time. By gathering data and designing lessons that are at the right starting point, we become not only effective teachers but efficient ones as well.

Reasons for Assessing Before Learning

- to determine students' differences *before* planning lessons
- to make decisions about the best options for differentiating for our students
- to get information about the interests, learning styles, and readiness levels of students
- to identify starting points for instruction
- to identify who already knows and who has gaps
- to allow for more efficient use of instructional time

Figure 14.1 How to Assess Before Learning

To Determine	Use	Examples and Information
How to best deliver and assess the content you are about to teach	Student learning styles profile	See Resources section for examples.
What interests and/or attitudes students have about the content you are about to teach	Content-related interest survey	See Resources section for examples.
What students know and understand about the content you are about to teach What misconceptions students might have about the content you are about to teach What critical thinking skills students currently possess	Quick write	Have students discuss, write, map, or draw what they think they already know before you begin.
	Teacher-prepared pretests for global concepts	Students who know 80 percent or above on a pretest should be given alternative work, such as an independent contract. Students with little or no background knowledge need to build more prior knowledge as they study the unit.
	Teacher observation checklists	Make a checklist of observable skills needed and check off your observations. Use the data to form focus learning groups.
	Students' product and work samples	Review a current piece of work, using your C U KAN framework, to look for indicators of what students already know, understand, or are able to do for an upcoming unit.
	Squaring off	Students can either move to signs posted in the room, or you can have them jot down their level and you can collect these. **Pro** – I know enough about this topic that I could teach it to others. **Top Player** – I know a lot, enough to know there's more. **Rookie** – I have some knowledge, but need to learn a lot more. **Amateur** – I don't know much about this topic.
	Anticipation guides	Students respond to a set of agree/disagree statements related to a lesson. Their predictions give indications of their background knowledge on the subject.
	Traffic light	Give students the objectives of the unit and either green, red, or yellow stickers or markers. If they think they know the objective well, they mark it green. If they have some knowledge, but not a lot, they mark the objective yellow. If they don't know much, they mark it red.

Assessment During Learning

Once we have established our learning objectives and preassessed our students, it is time to monitor their growth toward the targeted objectives. This is also the time to teach students to self-reflect on their own growth toward meeting the objectives. (See Figure 14.2.)

Assessment during learning gives us the data we need to keep our students on track, to adjust our teaching to what our students need, and to help students reflect on their learning. By using a four-finger assessment to check students' understanding of the vocabulary terms, Ms. Johnson gathers the data she needs for the next day's instruction, without burdening herself with a quiz to grade. Names of students who indicated a three or a four (need some review/haven't learned it yet) are jotted down on a sticky note. She will pull them into a small group the following day to review the terms while other students continue making progress on their research.

Reasons for Assessing During Learning

- to monitor and adjust students' work
- to give students feedback from us, their peers, and themselves
- to help students before the grading of a lesson or unit when it may be too late
- to help students realistically reflect on where they are in their understanding of the learning target

Figure 14.2   How to Assess During Learning

To Determine	Use	Examples and Information
If you need to adjust students' work If students need help before the grading of a lesson or unit (when it may be too late) If students are reflecting on what they know, understand, and are able to do	Kid watching	Teacher observes behaviors of students working on projects, takes notes, and provides feedback when appropriate. Sticky notes are great for giving immediate feedback. Students love to read the messages we write to them.
	High five	On a scale of 1–5, how well do I know this? (Students can jot the number down or hold up the number of fingers that shows where they are in their understanding.) • I could teach it to others. • I can do it on my own. • I need some help. • I could use more practice. • I am just learning this.
	Thumbs up!	Students raise thumbs up if they know a lot about what they are learning. Students turn thumbs sideways if they know some, but not all, about what they are learning. Students turn thumbs down if they know very little about what they are learning or if they are lost.
	Exit cards	Students fill out exit questionnaire cards, reflecting on where they are in understanding and knowing the learning objectives of the unit. Teachers read and assess.(See the Resources for exit card examples.)
	Traffic light	Same as in preassessment, but students add green, red, or yellow dots to show how they have grown in their learning since the preassessment.
	Quiz	We can give students a mini-quiz at various points in the unit. Students should assess themselves or each other and use the information from the quiz to reflect on what they know and still need to learn.

Assessment After Learning

Once the learning process is complete, we do a final assessment, or grade students, to measure how well they hit the learning target. (See Figure 14.3.)

Ms. Johnson makes sure to include a student self-reflection in her final assessment. By having students think about their own quality of work and growth toward an outcome, she is giving learners the opportunity to know themselves better as thinkers, as learners, and as workers.

Reasons for Assessing After Learning

- to find out what students have learned about a topic
- to teach students to reflect on their growth as learners
- to evaluate where students are in their thinking and learning

Figure 14.3   How to Assess After Learning

To Determine If Students	Use	Examples and Information

Have mastered facts Have memorized information or Can recall details	True/False Multiple choice tests Fill in the blank	1. What year did the _____ begin?
		  a.
		  b.
		  c.
		2. A decimal and a _____ represent the same proportion.

Have acquired thinking skills Can apply reasoning or Have developed a deep understanding	Open or constructed response Essay questions	1. What were major factors that influenced the beginning of the American Civil War? _____ 2. Compare and contrast *Romeo and Juliet* with *West Side Story*.
Have mastered a skill or ability Can structure and apply skills Have acquired thinking skills Can apply reasoning or Have developed a deep understanding	Performance-based demonstration of ability	**Choice Menu** Make a poster, present a lesson, or perform a skit. **Real Application** Send a persuasive letter to your member of Congress. Develop a marketing campaign to sell tickets for the junior talent show.
Recognize their own understanding of the learning Recognize their strengths	Student self-assessment, reflection, and goal setting	**Portfolios** Students collect work, usually in a folder, and periodically reflect on their progress over time, identifying evidence of growth and making a plan for future learning. **Student Led Conferences** Students plan a conference time to meet with parents and the teacher to discuss how they have learned. **Rubrics and Reflections on Quality of Work** What I did that was quality What I would do better next time

GRADING IN THE INSPIRING CLASSROOM: NOW THEY GET IT!

Grading is an important topic to consider as we learn to reach and teach all types of elementary learners. To gain clarity about the purpose for grading, there are questions we may want to ponder regarding what and how we measure students' learning.

If we grade to measure whether or not our students "got it," are we doing so in ways that are fair to all learners? Is it fair for us to expect our students to show understanding in the exact same way now that we clearly recognize that our students learn differently? Should our students be graded on individual growth or on a standard measure of achievement? Is it fair to compare a student with learning challenges to a student who is a gifted learner? Using traditional grading practices, it is possible for gifted students to get "As" without really trying hard or learning anything? At the same time, we have students with learning challenges who work their tails off only to receive a "D," when in truth, they have progressed more than the advanced student. So, does a single score really reflect our students' learning?

In the "real world" we need to gain knowledge, experience accomplishments, and develop a work ethic to succeed. So perhaps a more fair and equitable way to measure what students have learned would be to measure for three criteria: (1) how well a student has mastered the content, (2) how much progress a student has made, and (3) what work habits is a student developing.

Some visionary school districts are actually making the move toward powerful grading reform as suggested by Carol Ann Tomlinson and Jay McTighe in their book, *Integrating Differentiated Instruction + Understanding by Design* (2006). For example, Crystal Lake District 47, a suburb of Chicago, has based their electronic grading system on the following three sets of criteria: (1) progress—how much students have gained from their learning experience, (2) product—what students know and are able to do as related to the learning standards, and (3) process—what tools students are developing to make their learning gains (www.d47schools.org). This grading system allows teachers to clearly communicate whether students have made any growth from where they started; if they are functioning above, at, or below grade level; and if they are developing learning skills and habits of mind. A grading system like this offers students and parents far more useful feedback than a single grading system does.

If our districts have not yet made the major shift toward a more equitable, informative grading system, we can still begin to shift our own paradigm about grading. Here are some thoughts and suggestions as we move toward inspiring assessment and grading:

- We can use anecdotal narratives on our report cards or hold student-led conferences to communicate to parents where their child stands regarding content mastery, progress toward goals, and work habits.
- If we begin our units and lessons by developing our C U KAN framework, and clearly defining what we want students to Understand, Know, and Be Able To Do, then we can more effectively

design the Now You Get It component of our lessons to match that criteria. For example, we are able to design our choice menus much more effectively when we create them with the learning target in mind. Choice menus don't work very well when we design random, "fun" choices without first considering what we expect students to show in their final products.

- Balancing differentiated grades with traditional tests and assessments allows the top student to be at the top, but the struggling learner or weak test-taker does not always have to be at the bottom.

ASSESSING OUR OWN GROWTH

When we work to create the Inspiring Classroom, it's important that we also reflect upon and assess our own growth. As teachers, we have a tendency to be hard on ourselves. We often expect that our lessons should turn out right the first time. We also have limited time and energy for creating the perfect lesson to teach every day. How do we move ourselves forward, without beating ourselves up?

Here are some suggestions for getting started, for growing our skills, and for being patient with ourselves in the process.

Start small. You don't have to do it all. Start at your comfort level.

- Gather one piece of data about your students, and organize it into a user-friendly format. (See Chapter 3.)
- Implement some ideas from Chapter 3 to create the environment and set the tone in your classroom.
- Try some lite-n-lean strategies from Chapter 5. They are easy to do, and, when you see how much the students enjoy learning this way, you'll be motivated to try some of the more advanced designs.
- Design one deep-n-dynamic lesson per quarter from Chapter 6. These lessons do take time to design well. But if you set a goal to design one per quarter, you will start to build a repertoire of quality lessons. Design four more lessons the following year, and see your repertoire of engaging and meaningful lessons grow!

Collaborate with others.

- It's much more fun to write lessons and discuss ideas with other teachers.
- Set a goal to get together with colleagues once a quarter to write a C U KAN lesson or unit. Note how powerful your thinking and your lessons become when you put your heads together!

Make time for reflection.

- No matter how wise you are, or how long you've been teaching, you will go through five stages in learning to change and grow your

practice. There *will* be risk taking and mistake making involved. In learning to teach this way, all of us will grow through these stages:
- o unconsciously incompetent
- o consciously incompetent
- o consciously competent
- o unconsciously competent
- o reflective competence

- These lessons rarely come out right the first time you teach them. (Believe us, we speak from experience on this point!) When you try a lesson and it does not go well, rather than saying to yourself, "This doesn't work in my classroom," you can ask, "Hmmm, I really liked the way many of my students responded to this lesson, but what can I do to fix that management problem? Let me see. I think they would work in their groups better if I gave them jobs like leader and recorder. Then I think I need to have them make up a list of tasks needed to complete the project and have them commit to which part they are going to complete."
- The C U KAN lesson planner in the Resources has a built-in reflection section where you can jot down what you want to change for the next time. Building this simple reflective habit will have a great affect on growing your skills.

It's okay not to know, but once you know, it's *not* okay not to grow.

- If we expect our students to be risk takers, then we need to model risk taking ourselves. Now that we know some new techniques, we need to take a risk and try them out! We can have some fun with this. Remember, if *we* are having fun teaching, it is very likely that our students are having fun learning!

As we look at our students and envision the type of human beings we want them to be in this world, it is clear that they learn more from us than they do from simply learning facts and mastering skills. We are also helping them to be able to reflect on progress toward goals and to develop lifelong learning habits that empower them beyond school. In the inspiring classroom, we know we must have a way to report this information to our students, to show them we see their growth beyond the content standards. We recognize and honor the skills they are developing. If we don't, we are likely to lose them. Assessment and grading must recognize that students learn at different rates and show growth in many ways. This more encompassing and informative system honors all the ways that humans grow.

15

Learning to Grow an Inspiring Classroom

Here's to the crazy ones . . . the misfits, the rebels . . . the trouble-makers . . . the round pegs in the square holes . . . the ones who see things differently. They're not fond of rules. You can quote them, disagree with them, glorify or vilify them. But the only thing you can't do is ignore them, because they change things . . . they push the human race forward. And while some may see them as the crazy ones, we see genius. Because the ones who are crazy enough to think that they can change the world . . . are the ones who do.

—Steve Jobs

What does an Inspiring Classroom look like when we are putting all the pieces together? How does our classroom develop from a group of strangers who hardly know one another to a rich interactive community? If we peek into an Inspiring Classroom at various points of a school year, what would we see? What would we hear? How would it change in complexity throughout the year?

For two years, Heather Nuckolls, a fourth grade teacher, has been weaving the attributes of an Inspiring Classroom into her practice. She has given herself time and permission to hone her skills. Let's take a look at her classroom and four snapshot moments throughout the school year to see how her practice as well as her students' skills bloom and mature.

SEPTEMBER

We walk into Mrs. Nuckolls's room and see that students are seated on the floor for morning meeting. She finishes reading a short excerpt from *Chicken Soup for the Kid's Soul*. She asks students to respond to the reading "short and sweet" so that everyone can participate. One by one, students share a comment or simply say, "pass." Mrs. Nuckolls uses this time to personally greet each child by name.

For two weeks, the class has been focusing on setting personal and academic intentions for the day. After hearing the reading responses, Mrs. Nuckolls moves on to the next activity. "Thank you, class, for sharing your ideas and your wisdom with all of us. Let's set our intentions for the day."

The students immediately turn to a person sitting next to them and talk for thirty seconds each. We hear students share plans such as the following: "I'm going to work on my writing today and add better revisions to make it sound more like Donald Sobol." Or, "I'm going to stick with my partner at recess and avoid the soccer field." Or "I'm going to keep my cool." And even, "I'm going to keep my desk organized."

After one minute of sharing with each other, Mrs. Nuckolls asks the students to close their eyes. She reminds them that visualizing is a skill that many people use when they are trying to create something. "Readers visualize to create understanding, artists visualize to create ideas, and you, as a student, can visualize to help you create your day." She asks students to visualize their intentions in their minds and create positive feelings around that image. She closes the meeting with a simple phrase, "Let's see what we can create together today!"

OCTOBER

Mrs. Nuckolls is entering into the fourth week with her new class. The state standardized test is beginning the following week. She knows the importance of test review at the beginning of the year but not at the cost of honoring students, establishing community, and getting started practicing the vital know-hows.

On the walls there are various charts and graphs that reflect information about each student's learning styles. There are three charts above the chalkboard that are labeled "Chunk," "Chew," and "Check." Under each word is a list of the ways students can take in information, process information, or show what they know. There is also a chart describing the skills for discourse with reminders for students of what it looks like and what it sounds like when people are communicating effectively.

Mrs. Nuckolls decides that discourse is a great vital know-how to use for reviewing the major concepts in science for the upcoming state test. She knows this will not only help prepare them for the test but will be great for continuing to build community, honoring individual differences in learning styles, and practicing core group skills. She explains:

> Okay, class. Let's look at what we talked about yesterday. We have a lot of scientific information that we've remembered over the years!

Mrs. Nuckolls points to a chart where she has recorded a brainstorming session of science terms, facts, and ideas from the previous day.

> At this point, we have to find the *big ideas* that hold together all this stuff in our brains. When we find the big idea, we can group together the facts, terms, or other smaller ideas that go along with it. When we group information together like that, it helps us remember better. And that will be very helpful for you next week we are taking the BLEEP test.
>
> Last night I typed up a list of everything on this chart. We are going to work in our core groups to find the big ideas. Materials managers, you will get the list for your team. Team leaders, you will read through these directions and make sure everyone knows what to do (she places directions on the overhead), and team communicator, you will let me know if you have any questions.
>
> I'd like to give you a few reminders before we get started: We are working today to *chew* on information by talking with one another and sorting ideas. This is a great time to practice the vital know-how *discourse.* At the end of our work session when we share the big ideas your team discovered, I also want your team to talk about what you did to communicate effectively. Where should you look if you forget the key skills for discourse?

The class points to the chart labeled "Skills for Discourse."

> One last thing, you'll notice that for the *check* part of today's work, you will have to make a chart to show your big ideas. This is a good time to use the talents of the people in your group who have some art smart skills to make sure the chart is clear and easy to read.

After the students have processed their findings, Mrs. Nuckolls makes sure the students know why they are studying in various ways.

> We all know, the BLEEP test is coming up next week, and it is a test that uses your word smart intelligence. Let's review why it's important to review in a variety of ways . . .

Her students respond one by one, "Because some of us learn better in ways that aren't just word smart." "Because our brains are social!" "Because using *all* our smarts makes us *all* smarter."

Mrs. Nuckolls points to the three posters above the board and the class says in unison, *"Chunk, chew, and check! It's how our brains learn best!"* (See Figure 15.1.)

DECEMBER

It's early December and the year is in full swing. Mrs. Nuckolls's students have developed a strong community that honors one another and shares problem solving strategies during class meetings. She is implementing deep n dynamic designs in order to move her students toward the same learning objectives.

Figure 15.1   Bulletin Board: How Do You Learn Best?

She is now using a larger variety of grouping arrangements. The core groups still work together to review homework, help each other with missing work, and process class problems. Study buddies are another ongoing grouping strategy that she uses for tiering when she wants students to work with others of similar readiness. Sometimes she also uses learning styles groups when she wants students to review information with others that process like them.

She is using a two-day choice menu to assess students' skills at synthesizing text for deeper meaning.

Okay, class. We've been working on the comprehension skill "synthesizing information" and I think you're ready to "show what you know."

She places a choice menu on the overhead and continues:

Let's take a look at this choice menu for your project. As you can see you will be able to demonstrate your synthesizing skills in a way that fits your learning style. Let's look at what your project should contain . . .

In math, her students are working on adding and subtracting fractions. From previous years of experience, Mrs. Nuckolls knows this is an area where students differ greatly in their readiness. She has decided to tier her lessons for the next few days.

She opens each day with a short mini-lesson. In ten minutes, she connects to the previous day's lesson, gives the students direct instruction on a new skill, and summarizes by giving students directions for their work. Then she asks students to move to their study buddy groups. She moves first to the group that is most likely to struggle.

"I want this group to turn and talk about today's lesson. Use this to keep notes." She hands them an overhead pen and a laminated T-chart that reads "What we DO get" and "What was confusing." "I'll be right back to review this with you."

She moves to the second group and says, "Tony, will you summarize today's mini-lesson for the group? I want everyone else to listen to see if you agree. If everyone agrees, you can get started on today's work. I'll be back to see how you are doing. "

The last group she visits is the advanced group. "Today's work is pretty similar to yesterday's and I know you did well with that. Today, I want you to do the last five questions. When you have completed those, give me the signal and I'll come check your work. If you get it after those five, then you can all go work on your anchor activities."

She moves back to the first group of strugglers to see where they are stuck. "I see you have the first three steps down pretty good. Let's take a look at your next steps."

FEBRUARY

Mrs. Nuckolls has been weaving and layering aspects of an inspiring classroom into her instruction for half the year. She is now able to choose from the differentiated designs that will best meet her students' needs. There is a Big Idea bulletin board. (See Figure 15.2.)

Figure 15.2 Big Idea Bulletin Board

For each unit in each content area, the big idea is recorded on the board. When students make interdisciplinary connections, a string is tied from one big idea to another.

Mrs. Nuckolls finds tiering to be highly effective in math. She continues to tier her groups using study buddies especially in the area of computation.

In writing, Mrs. Nuckolls is using flexible grouping to teach writing strategies based on the specific needs of students. Some groups are working on exciting leads, some are learning to paragraph, while others are improving their word choice skills.

She has preassessed students' knowledge about Michigan history and found that two students have extensive knowledge and high interest in the topic. She has compacted the curriculum for them by designing an independent study tied to the same objectives but with more extensive research demands. These two students will be sharing their investigation with the class as the end of the unit. (See Figure 15.3.)

Figure 15.3 Self-Assess Michigan History

In science, the class is doing an investigation on mechanical systems. Mrs. Nuckolls created a whole class contract that allows students to develop independence and work at their own pace. The students who finish their daily tasks early are working on an ongoing anchor activity with more complex electrical systems.

These snapshots of Mrs. Nuckolls's classroom portray an ever-evolving and multifaceted learning environment. It is an environment that grows through small steps, continuous reflection, and giving yourself permission to be a learner as well as a teacher.

Reaping the Harvest

Creating an Inspiring Legacy

You are a child of the universe, no less than the trees and the stars; you have a right to be here.

—Max Ehrmann, *Desiderata*

A gardener toils over his garden for many months knowing there will be a bountiful and beautiful harvest as a reward for his labors. Like gardening, creating and teaching in an Inspiring Classroom is challenging, but the harvest is ultimately very rewarding. Why? Because we are doing what is educationally sound and right. We are not forgetting, despite the pressures of high-stakes testing, that our students deserve to be able to learn in a safe and inviting community. They have a right to be taught in ways that honor who they are. They should be taught information that is relevant to their lives.

So, as we begin to sow our garden of learners, let us be inspired by the faces that surround us. Be joyfully curious about who our students are. Be open to all the possibilities they bring to our learning community. Be willing to take risks and make mistakes with them to make learning come alive in our classrooms.

We create the harvest we reap in our classrooms. Will we grow learners who are inspired or complacent? The choice is ours. We can choose to experience the joy of knowing our students, the richness of learning in community, and the power of connecting students' lives to the depth of our content; or, we can choose to cover content and teach as if one size fits all. If we choose to pass along a legacy of inspiration, we lead our students to discover their own greatness. Because they have seen themselves as contributors in our Inspiring Classrooms, they will see themselves as contributors in creating a better world. And the world will be a better place. What greater harvest could we possibly reap?

You Are a Marvel

Each second we live in a new and unique moment of the universe, a moment that will never be again. . . .
And what do we teach our children?
We teach them that two times two makes four, and that Paris is the capitol of France.
When will we also teach them what they are?
We should say to each of them: Do you know what you are?
You are a marvel.
You are unique.
In all the years that have passed, there never was another child like you.
Your legs, your arms, your clever fingers, the way you move.
You may become a Shakespeare, a Michelangelo, a Beethoven.
You have the capacity for anything.
Yes, you are a marvel.
And when you grow up, can you then harm another who is like you, a marvel?
You must work, we must all work, to make the world worthy of its children.

—Pablo Cascals
(1876–1973)

Resources

HOW TO USE THE RESOURCES:

The Resources are designated by an alphabetical and numerical component. The alphabetical component represents a group of similar resources. For example, B.3 and B.5 are student surveys. The numerical component signifies the sequence within the group of similar items and helps navigate the reader through that section.

A. The Big Picture
   1. Overview
   2. Goal Setting

B. Student Surveys and Questionnaires
   1. Student Observation Inventory Grades K–2
   2. Multiple Intelligences Survey Grades 3–5
   3. Learning Styles Inventory Grades K–2
   4. Learning Styles Inventory Grades 3–5
   5. Environmental Learning
      Preferences Grades K–2
   6. Environmental Learning
      Preferences Grades 3–5
   7. Interest Survey Grades K–2
   8. Interest Survey Grades 3–5
   9. Content Specific Inventories

C. Resources for Working With Groups
   1. Group Work Contract
   2. Group Processing Sheets
   3. Group Behavior Chart

D. Bibliography for Vital Know-Hows

E. Templates for Vital Know-How Strategies
   1. Journal for Vocabulary Development
   2. Reflect/Pair/Share
   3. Learning Log Ideas
   4. Inquiry Guide

F. At-a-Glance
   1. Elementary Anchor Activities
   2. Ways to Chunk, Chew, and Check Learning
   3. Ways to Prime the Brain for Learning
   4. Differentiated Instruction (DI):
      Management Tips and Strategies

G. C U KAN
1. C U KAN Examples and Nonexamples of "Understandings"
2. C U KAN Learning Target Template
3. C U KAN Planning Guide Template
4. Sample C U KAN With Examples and Nonexamples of Choices

H. Lesson Templates
1. Tic-Tac-Toe
2. Cubing
3. RAFT Plus

I. Lesson Planning Guides and Example Handouts
1. Designing a Student Contract
2. Student Work Contract
3. Work Log (for Individuals or Groups)
4. Learning Stations
5. Curriculum Compacting

J. Assessment
1. Quality Work Self-Assessment
2. Station Exit Card: Self-Assessment
3. Quality Work Criteria
4. C U KAN Rubric Template
5. Early Elementary Rubric Template

K. Further Readings
1. General
2. Varied Level Texts

A.1 THE BIG PICTURE: OVERVIEW

Creating an Inspiring Classroom: Meeting the Needs of All Learners

Honor and Inspire	Build Community	Engaging & Meaningful Lessons
Gather data about your learners • Readiness • Learning Styles • Personal Interests & Content-Related Interests	**Physical Environment** Establish Procedures (not rules) for: ○ Material Usage ○ Space Usage ○ Class Operations ○ Class Meetings or Community Problem Solving	**Apprentice Students in Mastery of the Vital Know-Hows (VKHs) for Learning** • Collaboration/ Cooperation • Discourse • Reflective Thinking/Learning • Reading and Writing for Learning • Inquiry
	Emotional Environment • Use data to recognize each learner's unique qualities • Use student strengths to build positive interdependence • Establish a classroom message backed up by literature, analogies, modeling, and class themes	**Use Lite-n-Lean Strategies** to allow students to practice the VKHs while instructionally responding to learners' differences **Use Deep-n-Dynamic Designs** to teach state objectives and outcomes in a meaningful way according to students': • Readiness • Interests • Learning Styles

A.2 THE BIG PICTURE: GOAL SETTING

Honor and Inspire	Build Community	Engaging & Meaningful Lessons
Gather data about your learners Goal:	**Physical Environment** Goal:	**Apprentice Students in Mastery of the Vital Know-Hows (VKHs) for Learning** Goal:
	Emotional Environment Goal:	**Use Lite-n-Lean Strategies** Goal: **Use Deep-n-Dynamic Designs** Goal:

B.1 STUDENT OBSERVATION INVENTORY GRADES K–2

Observe and record information about your students' learning styles, learning preferences, and multiple intelligences.

Student	Work Habits	Learning Profiles and Strengths	Learning Challenges	I can honor his/her learning needs by trying:

B.2 MULTIPLE INTELLIGENCES SURVEY GRADES 3–5

How Are You Smart?

Everyone is smart in several ways. This survey helps you understand what strengths you have. Some of us are really smart in one or two ways. Some of us are really smart in many ways. It is important to highlight our strengths (when doing projects, homework assignments, or working in groups). And it is also a lot of fun and a great challenge to work on those areas where we feel we aren't so smart—we will be strengthening our weaknesses. Directions: Check off the items that are most like you.

A
- ☐ I like to tell jokes.
- ☐ I like to read.
- ☐ I like to make up stories and tales.
- ☐ I write easily and enjoy it.
- ☐ I like crosswords and word games.

B
- ☐ I solve math problems easily.
- ☐ I enjoy using computers.
- ☐ I like to solve logic puzzles.
- ☐ I enjoy strategy games.

C
- ☐ People ask me for advice.
- ☐ I prefer team sports.
- ☐ I have many close friends.
- ☐ I am comfortable in a crowd.
- ☐ I like working in groups.

D
- ☐ I enjoy musical selections.
- ☐ I remember many tunes.
- ☐ I listen to music when studying.
- ☐ I enjoy singing.
- ☐ I am sensitive to tones and sounds.

E
- ☐ I know about my feelings, strengths, and weaknesses.
- ☐ I like to learn more about myself.
- ☐ I enjoy being alone sometimes.
- ☐ I enjoy hobbies by myself.
- ☐ I have confidence in myself.

F
- ☐ I see clear pictures in my mind.
- ☐ I am interested in color and design.
- ☐ I can find my way in new places.
- ☐ I draw and doodle.
- ☐ I prefer books with charts, graphs, and maps.

G
- ☐ I am a "touchy feely" person.
- ☐ I use my hands a lot when I talk.
- ☐ I enjoy hobbies using my hands.
- ☐ I think I am well coordinated.
- ☐ I learn better by doing than by watching.

H
- ☐ I like to categorize things.
- ☐ I see details in nature.
- ☐ I can hear animal and bird sounds clearly.
- ☐ I enjoy gardening and/or pets.
- ☐ I can identify trees, birds, plants.

(Continued)

(Continued)

B.2 MULTIPLE INTELLIGENCES SURVEY GRADES 3–5

Your Unique Multiple Intelligence Profile

Directions:

1. Count the total number of checked items in each category from the "How are you smart?" survey above. Fill in one cube in each row for the number of checks in each category. For example: In the E category (Self Smart), if you have 3 checks, color in 3 boxes in the horizontal row next to Self Smart.

2. The bar graph will create a snapshot to help you understand your areas of strength and help you identify areas that you may need to target for growth.

Number of Checked Items:	1	2	3	4	5
A – Word Smart					
B – Math Smart					
C – People Smart					
D – Music Smart					
E – Self Smart					
F – Picture Smart					
G – Body Smart					
H – Nature Smart					

What are you currently good at? _____

_____

What is something you can do in the classroom with your unique strengths to help others?

_____

_____

What area might you consider working on for improvement?

_____

What is one thing you can do in the classroom to work on that type of smart?

_____

B.3 LEARNING STYLES INVENTORY GRADES K–2

When I learn something new, I do best when I:

talk about it

hear about it

read about it

write about it

work with it

think about it

(Continued)

(Continued)

B.3 LEARNING STYLES INVENTORY GRADES K–2

When I need to understand directions in class, I do best when I:

tell a friend the directions

read the directions

write down the steps

"see" the steps in my mind

listen closely to the teacher

figure it out by doing it

B.4 LEARNING STYLES INVENTORY GRADES 3–5

Learning styles are the ways that we are able to take in and make sense of new information. Of the six different learning styles, most people have one or two that are their strengths. However, you may have a combination of several styles that you use for learning. Answer each question below with the response that *best* describes how you take in and think about new information.

_____ 1. To make sense of new learning, it helps me to
   a. talk about it
   b. think about it
   c. read about it
   d. write about it
   e. hear about it
   f. work with it

_____ 2. I do best in classes where teachers
   a. let me work in small groups and talk over ideas with others
   b. let me have some quiet time to think about the new information
   c. let me read about new information before lectures
   d. let me write down my thoughts and questions
   e. lecture on new information
   f. design an activity for me to do; draw, construct, experiment

_____ 3. If I need to get directions to a new place, I prefer to
   a. repeat the directions verbally
   b. see the map in my mind
   c. read the written directions
   d. write the directions down for myself
   e. listen to someone give me directions
   f. grab a map and figure it out

_____ 4. If the teacher draws a diagram on the board, I make sense of it by
   a. talking about it with a friend
   b. seeing the picture
   c. reading some text that discusses the concept
   d. writing down the major ideas
   e. remembering what the teacher said about it
   f. drawing it for myself

_____ 5. If I need to learn how to spell a new word, I will
   a. say it over and over again to myself
   b. visualize the letters in my mind
   c. look at it on paper
   d. write it a few times
   e. spell it out loud to hear if it sounds right
   f. use my fingers to trace the letters in the air

(Continued)

(Continued)

B.4 LEARNING STYLES INVENTORY GRADES 3–5

Graph and Interpretation

Grab your colored pencils and lets "see" what you discovered about yourself. Count how many As, Bs, Cs, etc. you have from the above survey. Color in the corresponding number of blocks in each column. Remember, some columns may have no bars in them! Then read about your strength areas below the graph.

5						
4						
3						
2						
1						
	A Speaking	B Visualizing	C Reading	D Writing	E Listening	F Manipulating

Looking at the bar graph above, you can see which learning style is your strongest (usually three or more). If it is A, **speaking**, you learn best by expressing yourself out loud. If it is B, **visualizing,** you learn best when you have a picture in your mind. If it is C, **reading, i**t is easy for you to read about things and remember and understand them. If it is D, **writing,** you express yourself easily through writing. If it is E, **listening, i**t is easy for you to acquire new information by hearing it. And if it is F, **manipulating,** you learn best by manipulating objects and moving things around.

If no letter occurred more than the others, you have a balanced learning style and can acquire and process information in many ways.

Honor the way you learn. When you are given a choice of how to take in new information, use this knowledge of the strengths you have and use your learning style to own the new learning!

B.5 ENVIRONMENTAL LEARNING
PREFERENCES GRADES K–2

**Circle the picture in each pair that describes
the environment that you like to learn in.**

1. Quiet   Loud

2. Desk   Floor

3. Group   Alone

4. Sitting   Moving

5. With Help   With No Help

B.6 ENVIRONMENTAL LEARNING
PREFERENCES GRADES 3–5

How Do You Like To Learn?

1.	I study best when it is quiet.	Yes	No
2.	I am able to ignore the noise of other people talking while I am working.	Yes	No
3.	I like to work at a table or desk.	Yes	No
4.	I like to work on the floor.	Yes	No
5.	I work hard for myself.	Yes	No
6.	I work hard for my parents or teacher.	Yes	No
7.	I will work on an assignment until it is completed, no matter what.	Yes	No
8.	Sometimes I get frustrated with my work and do not finish it.	Yes	No
9.	When my teacher gives an assignment, I like to have exact steps on how to complete it.	Yes	No
10.	When my teacher gives an assignment, I like to create my own steps on how to complete it.	Yes	No
11.	I like to work by myself.	Yes	No
12.	I like to work in pairs or in groups.	Yes	No
13.	I like to have an unlimited amount of time to work on an assignment.	Yes	No
14.	I like to have a certain amount of time to work on an assignment.	Yes	No
15.	I like to learn by moving and doing.	Yes	No

B.7 INTEREST SURVEY GRADES K–2

What I Like

Circle five of your favorite things to do.

I like to count.

I like to draw.

I like books.

I like to invent things.

I like to be with others.

I like to act things out.

I like to listen to stories.

I like to collect and sort things.

I like to build things.

I like to dance and move.

I like to work alone.

I like to help others.

B.8 INTEREST SURVEY GRADES 3–5

Personal Interest Inventory

1. What is your favorite subject to learn about in school? (Check all that apply)

☐ Writing   ☐ Geography
☐ Reading   ☐ History
☐ Physical Education   ☐ Science
☐ Art   ☐ Math
☐ Literature   ☐ Computers
☐ Other: _____

2. What do you enjoy the most about school? What do you enjoy the least about school?
   _____
   _____

3. Do you prefer to work   A. Alone   B. In groups   C. Both (Circle One)

4. What hobbies and special interests do you have (e.g., sports, clubs, collections, activities)? Be specific.
   _____
   _____

5. What do you like to do when you have free time?
   _____
   _____

6. How much time do you spend watching TV each week? _____
   What do you watch?
   _____

7. How much time do you spend on the computer each week? _____
   What do you like to do on the computer?
   _____

8. What types of music do you listen to? _____

9. What should a teacher know about you that will help you learn best in school?
   _____

10. What is the most important thing to you in your life? What are your future goals? _____
    _____

11. What is something that you do really well and that you are most proud of?
    _____
    _____

B.9 CONTENT SPECIFIC INVENTORIES

Science – Simple Machines

Rank these categories (1 = top choice) to show what you are most interested in studying during our unit on Simple Machines. How simple machines are used in:

____ Art

____ Sports

____ Entertainment

____ Music

____ History

____ Math

Geography – Introduction to Elements

What are you most interested in?

____ Maps and Globes

____ Cultures

____ Physical systems

____ Data (demographics, shifts, etc.)

Rate the following in order of personal enjoyment using 1 (high) through 3 (low)

____ Create models and maps of land features.

____ Research and report how land features have changed over time.

____ Portray how societies have been affected by changes in land features.

Math – Operations

If you had to explain math operations (multiplication) to a partner in class, which way are you most interested in showing what you know?

____ Develop a story that illustrates multiplication.

____ Use a number line to demonstrate multiplication.

____ Draw a picture illustrating multiplication.

____ Explain the steps in solving multiplication problems.

C.1 GROUP WORK CONTRACT

This contract is hereby entered into by:

_____   _____

_____   _____

on this day, _____ .

We hereby call ourselves _____ .

Certain responsibilities and expectations come along with the opportunity to work closely with our peers. Some of these responsibilities and expectations include:

1. _____

2. _____

3. _____

4. _____

In addition to the above-mentioned, we each will be a critical part of the team and have committed to fulfilling one of the following roles:

* Team Coach _____

This person has the important role of keeping the team on track. She/he should keep the group on task, make sure every person understands what the assignment is, and ask questions when the assignment is not clear. Of primary importance: At the beginning of each class period see that every person in your group is filling out their agenda based on the class agenda at the front of the room.

* Materials Manager _____

This responsible and organized person should complete three main goals: (1) before class begins, gather materials for the team that the teacher has set up for the day's lesson; (2) pass out corrected work or papers from the class period folder; (3) turn in papers for the group including homework, tests, or work the teacher would like to see for the day.

C.1 GROUP WORK CONTRACT

* **Record Keeper** _____

This person should be an excellent summarizer who is capable of recording details. You will (1) maintain notes on the group work log; (2) record the groups' task list for the next day's work; (3) organize the group processing sheets or group behavior chart, whichever your group chooses to use.

* **Group Reporter** _____

A person of strong moral character and excellent communication skills should be assigned to this position. This person is responsible for maintaining the make-up folder for your group; which will include (1) daily notes from the Record Keeper of the team; (2) extra worksheets or copies for missing team members; (3) group processing sheets or behavior chart. Also, you will meet with me to discuss how your group is doing and share your group processing sheets/behavior chart.

I, _____ , have entered this agreement with trust. I have placed much responsibility upon each of you to help make this class a first-rate class. If there are any issues within your group that you cannot *first* resolve among yourselves, then please see me and we will work it out together. I trust that you will contribute your part. If you feel that you cannot carry out your responsibility, speak up in your group before signing your name.

About once a week, we will rate ourselves as to how your team is functioning. If all is going well, you may choose to keep the same person doing the same job. If, however, you see someone is not upholding *this* contract that *they* agreed to, then you may switch positions. Good luck!

Signed _____

Date _____

C.2 GROUP PROCESSING SHEETS

Group Processing Sheet

I completed my group job today.	Yes	No
I contributed ideas to the group.	Yes	No
I helped others if they needed my assistance.	Yes	No
I worked my best to solve problems with others.	Yes	No

Group Processing Sheet

I completed my group job today.	Yes	No
I contributed ideas to the group.	Yes	No
I helped others if they needed my assistance.	Yes	No
I worked my best to solve problems with others.	Yes	No

Group Processing Sheet

I completed my group job today.	Yes	No
I contributed ideas to the group.	Yes	No
I helped others if they needed my assistance.	Yes	No
I worked my best to solve problems with others.	Yes	No

Group Processing Sheet

I completed my group job today.	Yes	No
I contributed ideas to the group.	Yes	No
I helped others if they needed my assistance.	Yes	No
I worked my best to solve problems with others.	Yes	No

C.3 GROUP BEHAVIOR CHART

Name of Group:

After determining your group expectations for this task, rate your group from 1–5 each day for each group behavior. (One is the lowest, five is the highest.)

How did our group do today?	Date:	Date:	Date:	Date:	Date:

D. BIBLIOGRAPHY FOR VITAL KNOW-HOWS

Billmeyer, R., & Barton, M. I. (1998). *Teaching reading in the content areas: If not me, then who?* Aurora, CO: McRel.

Daniels, H., & Zemelman, S. (2004). *Subjects matter: Every teacher's guide to content area reading.* Portsmouth, NH: Heinemann Press.

Harvey, S., & Goudis, A. (2000). *Strategies that work.* York, ME: Stenhouse Publishers.

Horowitz, R. (Ed.). (1994). *Classroom talk about text: What teenagers and teachers come to know about the world through talk about text.* San Antonio, TX: International Reading Association.

Jensen, E. (1998). *Teaching with the brain in mind.* Alexandria, VA: Association for Supervision and Curriculum Development.

National Research Council. (2000). *How people learn: Brain, mind, experience and school.* Washington, DC: National Academy Press.

Reading next: A vision for action and research in middle and high school literacy. The Carnegie Corporation of New York and the Alliance for Excellence in Education. Retrieved May 7, 2006, from http://www.all4ed.org/publications/ ReadingNext/index.html.

Rothstein, E., & Lauber, G. (2000). *Writing as learning.* Arlington Heights, IL: Skylight Professional Development.

Schoenbach, R., Greenleaf, C., & Hurwitz, L. (1999). *Reading for understanding: A guide to improving reading in middle and high school classrooms.* San Francisco: Jossey-Bass.

Senost, R., & Thiese, S. (2001). *Reading and writing across content areas.* Arlington Heights, IL: Skylight Professional Development.

E.1 JOURNAL FOR VOCABULARY DEVELOPMENT

Word:

My Understanding			
? *I don't really understand it yet.*	☺ *I have some ideas.*	⬜ *I understand it.*	⬜*!!!!* *I can teach it to others.*

My Learning	
In my own words:	Pictures that help me:

Other connections I am making:

E.2 REFLECT/PAIR/SHARE

Question or Prompt	My Thoughts	Partner's Thoughts	Group Share

Possible Questions or Prompts:

What is the reason for this?

What evidence do I notice?

Is this working? If yes, why? If no, why not?

What do I think is important about this? Why?

What do I think is not important about this? Why?

What do I like about this? Why?

What do I not like about this? Why?

Why do I think the author did this?

When I am confused, I . . .

I am feeling really good about . . .

E.3 LEARNING LOG IDEAS

Encourage students to not only write in their learning logs, but to also draw, chart, map, and paste things into their logs.

Generic Questions to Guide Student Thinking:
(Free Response, Structured Response,
Habits of Mind, Content Probe, Learning)

- Quick Writes: Asking students to write nonstop for 3–5 minutes on a topic. Quick writes can be used for pre-, during-, and post-assessment, as a way to engage the class, as a way to generate dialogue, etc.
- What did I learn today?
- What did I understand well/feel most confident about?
- What is still confusing to me?
- What's the biggest problem you are having on your project?
- Explain what you have been doing to use resources more effectively.
- What did I find interesting?
- Explain what I did in class today.
- What was I supposed to understand from this lesson/unit?
- What connections did I make to previous ideas we have learned?
- Describe and give examples of new terms.
- What strategies did I use to help me learn this?
- Create a graphic representation of what I learned.
- Give evidence to support your thinking.
- Evaluate . . .
- Compare ideas or concepts.
- Predict what would have or will happen if. . .
- Defend your position.

Math:

- Explain to another student how to do the math problems. Include the "why" of the solution, not just the "how."
- Describe another way to look at this problem. You may need to talk to another student to get some ideas.

Social Studies:

- Write about the event from the perspective of someone who was there. Tell the who, what, when, where, how, and what if.
- Write a dialogue between myself and a person who was there.
- Describe one of the five themes of geography regarding this place.

Science:

- Observe and write, draw, or chart observations.
- Explain the process of . . .

Language Arts:

- Describe a character (or setting, theme, conflict, etc.).
- Observe and write observation. Now practice a specific writer's trick while writing about my observations.

E.4 INQUIRY GUIDE

Know What do I think I know about this topic?	*Wonder* What are some wonderings I have about this topic?	*How* Where will I look or go to find the answers?	*Learned* What did I find out?

F.1 ELEMENTARY ANCHOR ACTIVITIES

Language Arts	Math
• Silent reading • Journaling • Guinness Book Scavenger Hunt • Brain Quest • Create own Brain Quest questions • Word analogy games and puzzles • Word Wall Bulletin Board • Free computer time • Fluency tests • Write Jingles – to help recall content • Create Magnetic Poetry • Mad-gabs or Mad-libs • Word Sorts (parts of speech) • Sentence sequencing	• Create test questions/Story problems • Do "Problems of the Week" • Create a folder of review activities • Create a folder of problem solving activities • Puzzles and math games • Create math games • Manipulatives • Magazines (have kids connect articles to math) • Extended activities/Module project • Math journal writing • Research a math topic • Computer programs • Practice budgeting (holiday shopping, check book, weekly allowance)
Social Studies	**Science**
• Create vocabulary flash cards • Map activities • Board games • Create brochures guides • Summarize chapters in FUN ways (TV Guide) • Independent reading (Historical Fiction) • Create a mini-activity menu • Create a crossword puzzle • Journal • Write a song to help you learn • Brain Teasers • Design a monument • Create a play or skit • Write a biography about your historic hero	• Mini-lab centers • Science "Question of the Week" • Learning log • Read science articles • Create a mini-experiment • Science puzzles and games • Draw vocabulary pictures • Create a review game • Act out vocabulary • Add to "Science in the News" board • Write content songs • Add illustrated words to the word wall • Add to class timeline • Write scientist biographies

(Continued)

(Continued)

F.1 ELEMENTARY ANCHOR ACTIVITIES

Miscellaneous	Individual Inquiry
• Games and puzzles • Reading • Logic activities • Analogy activities • Mapping • Graphing • Computer Time	• Computer search • Novel/Short story writing • Research project • Life Plan project • Social action project • Career planning • Hobby or passion
Music/Art	Physical Education
• Play piano with headphones • Create new rhythm pattern • Read "Music Alive" or art articles • Create rap or song or visual mnemonic for another content area • Create a new melody (choose instrument) • Research favorite music or art	• Practice sports drills • Walk or jog • Do stretches • Yoga or aerobics • Research a PE or health topic • Meditate

F.2 WAYS TO CHUNK, CHEW, AND CHECK LEARNING

Chunk, Chew, and Check
(That's how the brain learns best!)

Chunk (Input): Varying the ways students acquire new information.

- Read the book or other outside text
- Do a role play
- Play a game
- Watch a video
- See a presentation or demonstration
- Do an experiment
- Use technology/media
- Class discussion
- Tiered Content – Content offered at varying readiness levels

Chew (Process): Varying learning activities or strategies to provide appropriate methods for students to explore the new concepts. It is important to give students alternative paths to process the ideas embedded within the concept.

- Do the questions
- Students design questions and share with each other
- Walk and talk about question prompts presented by the teacher
- Talk partners – students turn and talk to deepen understanding
- Total physical response – students learn or create movements to help them recall
- Tiered activities where students work at different levels of support, challenge, or complexity
- Centers that allows students to explore the key understandings in a variety of ways
- Developing contracts (task lists written by the teacher and containing both in-common work for the whole class and work that addresses individual needs of learners) to be completed either during specified agenda time or as students complete other work early
- Offering manipulatives or other hands-on supports for students who need them
- Using graphic organizers, maps, diagrams, or charts to display comprehension of concepts covered. Varying the complexity of the graphic
- Offering students a choice in how they want to process understanding of new vocabulary   (draw, map, act out, etc.)

Check (Output): Varying how students show understanding and transfer of the learning.

- Take a quiz or test
- Tiered products or tiered quiz/tests
- Product Choice (i.e., Song/Rap/Poem, Skit/Video, Presentation, etc.)
- Using rubrics that match and extend students' varied skills levels
- Allowing students to work alone or in small groups on their products
- Formative ongoing assessments with students involved in self-assessing

F.3 WAYS TO PRIME THE BRAIN FOR LEARNING

- KWL

- Make Predictions

- Anticipation Guides

- PowerPoint Presentations

- Video Clips

- Linking by Mapping/Webbing

- Posters

- Mixed Media

- Overhead

- Hands-on Materials

- Games

- Group Discussion

- Book Walk/Picture Walk

- Tell a story that relates to make a connection

- Give Objectives or Goals

- Link with what you did the day before

- Think/Pair/Share

- Guided Imagery

- Smell

- Touch (Props, experiments, manipulatives)

- Internet Search

- Poetry

- Story

F.4 DIFFERENTIATED INSTRUCTION (DI): MANAGEMENT STRATEGIES AND TIPS

Beginning of the Year Strategies to Prepare for a DI Classroom

- Set the classroom tone for differentiating
    - Gather student data and create Learning Profile Cards
    - Establish routines for
        - moving to Anchor Activities
        - collecting papers
        - discussing with learning partners
        - moving into groups
        - sharing ideas

- **Finishing Projects**
    - Create three sided table tents labeled Hard at Work, Help!, and Finished. (Be sure to check the finished work to see if it is quality work before allowing students to move to anchor activities.)
    - Use the same idea as above, only use red, yellow, and green plastic cups to indicate that students are working just fine (green), stuck and in need of help (red), or finished (yellow).

- **Chunk and Chew**
    - Do whole group instruction in small chunks (20 minutes or less) and then let students "chew" or process what they learned in appropriate small group or individual activities.

- **Brain Breaks** (Approximately every twenty minutes learners' brains need a break; time to process what they've learned.)
    - Stretches
    - Cross Laterals (arms and/or legs crossing over the body)
    - Energizers
    - Walk and talk (or just walk!)
    - Settling time
    - Music and movement

- **Ways to Process Learning**
    - Walk and talk (walk five giant steps and share)
    - Make a Date Clock Partners

(Continued)

(Continued)

F.4 DIFFERENTIATED INSTRUCTION (DI): MANAGEMENT STRATEGIES AND TIPS

○ Mapping/KWLs
○ Find someone who... (Pick a trait, i.e., shoe size, birth day)
○ Four Corners (Move to corners by traits, interests, or readiness)
○ Timed-Pair-Share
○ Rally Robin – groups of four, go out and learn from other group, come back and share with your group

- **Group Management Ideas**

  ○ *Always* monitor groups by floating and asking questions. Help students troubleshoot. Refrain from giving solutions.
  ○ Use a clipboard as you move through the room to monitor student performance.
  ○ As students are working in groups, write notes to them on sticky notes to provide them with quick feedback without interrupting the group process.
  ○ Appoint jobs in the groups for each group member (Possible Jobs: Leader, Recorder, Time Keeper, Teacher Getter, Positive Thinker, Organizer).
  ○ With students, develop expectations for working in groups. Create a rubric of criteria and have each group assess themselves at the end of each group work session. You then go around the room and agree or disagree with groups' self-assessment. You're the "boss," so your assessment counts. (Possible Expectations: On Task, Sharing Ideas, Cooperating, Using Time Wisely.)
  ○ Students who aren't working well in their groups, even after you have given warnings, should be "fired" from the group and given an alternative assignment to complete.

- **Miscellaneous Management Ideas**

  ○ The more responsibility students have for their own learning process, the more they will manage themselves.
  ○ Appoint Classroom Managers/Resident Experts.
  ○ See three before me! Students aren't allowed to come and ask you for help until they have checked with three other students in the room first.
  ○ Rehearse directions for new learning formats with the whole class before asking students to carry them out in differentiated groups.

G.1 C U KAN EXAMPLES AND NONEXAMPLES OF "UNDERSTANDINGS"

As you design your C U KAN lessons, it helps to use this chart to compare examples of understandings with the nonexamples of understandings.

Examples	Nonexamples
Students will understand that examining the similarities and differences between cultures strengthens the fabric of a multicultural society.	Students will understand the culture of Latin America.
Students will understand that writers let us into their characters' minds, so we can learn how internal conflicts can be handled in positive or negative ways.	Students will understand the plot, characters, and internal conflict in *The Gift of the Magi.*
Students will understand that scientists look for order and patterns to help them understand the nature of all things.	Students will understand the periodic table.
Students will understand that mathematicians look for the most efficient ways to solve problems.	Students will understand how to solve algebraic equations.
Students will understand that artists see an inanimate object from their perspective and create the image that *they* envision.	Students will understand how to paint a still life.
Students will understand that we can make sense of new content by understanding the meaning of key vocabulary.	Students will understand the key vocabulary words.

G.2 C U KAN LEARNING TARGET TEMPLATE

C U KAN LESSON DESIGN **LEARNING TARGET**

Concept (Overarching Theme):

As a result students should . . .

Understand (Key Principles):

Know (Facts):

Able To Do (Skills):

G.3 C U KAN PLANNING GUIDE TEMPLATE

PLANNING GUIDE
Preassess: How will you determine students' readiness, interests, or learning profiles before starting your lesson/unit?
Prime: How will you engage the learners at the beginning of the lesson/unit?
Where will you be differentiating instruction? Explain how you are differentiating as you describe that section of your lesson. ❑ Chunk/Information Acquired ❑ Chew/Information Processed ❑ Check/Information Out ❑ Content/The Information **Will you be using a dynamic design for differentiating instruction? If so, which design?** ❑RAFT Plus ❑Choice Designs ❑Tiered ❑Contract ❑Compacting ❑Centers
Chunk: How will students acquire the new learning?
Chew: How will students get to process the new learning?
Ongoing Assessment: How will you and/or students assess during the learning?
Now You Get It!/Check for Understanding: How will students show transfer of learning?
The Information: (Materials, Books, Web sites, etc.)

G.4 SAMPLE C U KAN WITH EXAMPLES AND NONEXAMPLES OF CHOICES

Understand: Authors write stories to teach us about life. We can learn about how to live our own life from stories.

Know:

- Ten new vocabulary words from *Freak the Mighty*, by Rodman Philbrick
- The theme of the story (message about life)
- Plot outline

Able To Do:

- Summarize key ideas
- Make personal connections to the text

Now You Get It! Choose one option from the menu below to show what you understand and know about *Freak the Mighty*. Include something in your project that shows what this story taught you about life.

Write a rap/poem/song about a character. What did you learn about life from that character?	Create, by drawing or building, something that represents what you learned from this story. Explain your art in writing or in speaking.
Create a comic book that has a theme or message similar to the theme in *Freak the Mighty*.	Make a character analysis chart. Note the main characters, their characteristics, and what they learned from the story. Plan to summarize the chart in writing or verbally.
Write and present a skit that re-creates the theme from *Freak*, or is perhaps a future scene from Freak's life that relates to the theme.	Write a reflection comparing yourself to Freak. How you are alike? How are you different? What did you learn about life from Freak that can help you in your life?

Choose one character and write a poem about that character.	Draw plans for an ornithopter and/or build an ornithopter.
Illustrate a scene from the book, using paint, markers, colored paper, or collage.	Find an actual medical diagnosis for Kevin. Write two or three paragraphs outlining how you found the diagnosis and why you think the diagnosis you found is correct.
Act out a scene from the book. You may work with one or more partners.	Kevin has his own dictionary of words and terms he has adopted or made up. Create your own dictionary with words and definitions.

H.1 LESSON TEMPLATE: TIC-TAC-TOE

Template: Choice Menu

Understand: _____

Know: _____

Able To Do: _____

Now You Get It!: _____

1.	2.	3.
4.	5.	6.
7.	8.	9.

Directions: Choose activities in a tic-tac-toe design. When you have completed the activities in a row—horizontally, vertically, or diagonally—you may decide to be finished. Or you may decide to keep going and complete more activities.

I choose activities # _____, # _____, # _____, # _____.

Do you have ideas for alternate activities you'd like to do instead? Talk them over with your teacher.

I prefer to do the following alternate activities: _____

_____

Name: _____

Date Received: _____ Date Due: _____

Date Completed: _____

H.2 LESSON TEMPLATE: CUBING

Understand:

Know:

Able To Do:

H.3 LESSON TEMPLATE: RAFT PLUS

Understand:

Know:

Able To Do:

Role:
Audience:
Format:
Task (Activity):

I.1 PLANNING GUIDE: DESIGNING A STUDENT CONTRACT

_____ Use the learning target to develop outcomes. Ask yourself . . .

    ☐ Does each choice align with the Understand, Know, and Do?

    ☐ Are these activities expanding upon the core activities that all students must complete?

    ☐ Is there a balance of outcomes for various learning styles?

    ☐ How will each task be weighted?

_____ Create a list of conditions the student/s agree to accept in the contract. Ask yourself . . .

    ☐ Am I holding them accountable if they do not fulfill their obligations?

    ☐ Are working habits and skills needed to complete the contract clear?

_____ Develop a plan of action with the student/s for each day's work session. Ask yourself . . .

    ☐ Does the student have all necessary materials?

    ☐ Have arrangements been made for the student to work in other areas of the school?

_____ Students and the teacher must sign the contract. You may also decide to have parents sign the contract.

_____ Determine how you will assess the student/s throughout the process and how you will assess yourself and the contract design at the end. Ask yourself . . .

    ☐ What worked? What didn't work?

    ☐ What management strategies need to change?

    ☐ What further planning do I need to do to improve the next contract?

I.2 EXAMPLE: STUDENT WORK CONTRACT

Student Name: _____

Having tested out of a unit, I promise to do the following:

1. I will select and complete an alternative assignment.

2. I will use my time wisely and keep track of the work I completed each day on the "Goal-Setting Log."

3. If I need help, I will wait until the teacher is not busy.

4. If no one can help, I will try to keep working or move to another activity.

5. I will not bother other students or the teacher.

6. I will not brag about working on an alternative assignment to other students.

7. I will complete the projects I choose to do and turn them in to the teacher.

Student Signature: _____

I agree to help the student follow this plan.

Teacher Signature: _____

Date: _____

I.3 TEMPLATE: WORK LOG (FOR INDIVIDUALS OR GROUPS)

Date:	Daily Work Plan:	Work Actually Completed:

I.4 PLANNING GUIDE: LEARNING STATIONS

Concept:

Understand:

Know:

Able To Do:

Accountability:

Will students be:
- o keeping a daily work log?
- o completing exit cards at each station?
- o doing a "partner progress" check?
- o turning in work along the way?
- o self-reflecting on progress (scale of 1–5; how to make improvements)?
- o Other?

Station 1 Title:

Objectives Met:

Materials Needed:

Structured or Exploratory Activity:

Station 2 Title:

Objectives Met:

Materials Needed:

Structured or Exploratory Activity:

Station 3 Title:

Objectives Met:

Materials Needed:

Structured or Exploratory Activity:

I.5 PLANNING GUIDE: CURRICULUM COMPACTING

1. Subject Area Being Studied: _____

2. Pretesting Method:

3. Options for Alternative Work:

   _____ a. Activity Extension Menu

   _____ b. Independent Project

   _____ c. Other

4. Expectations for Regular Unit Instruction

   _____ a. Unit quizzes and/or final

   _____ b. Unit special events

   _____ c. Subject matter not passed on pretest

5. Record Keeping

   _____a. Compacting Contract

   _____b. Daily Work Log

   _____c. Daily Exit Cards

   _____d. Evaluation Contract

J.1 QUALITY WORK SELF-ASSESSMENT

Name _____ Unit _____ Date _____

Quality Skill	Super	Standard	So-So	Slipped
Listening to Discussions and Directions				
Understanding Key Concepts				
Taking Complete/ Organized Notes				
Completing Warm-Ups				
Asking Questions When You Need to Know More				
Being Responsible During Lab Work				
Completing Homework Studying for Test				

Put a star next to the categories above in which you feel you did *Quality Work*.

Below list the categories in which you need to improve your *Quality*.

Are you willing to improve your *Quality* in any of these areas? If so, which areas and what will you do to improve your quality?

Area: _____ Improvement: _____

Area: _____ Improvement: _____

J.2 STATION EXIT CARD: SELF-ASSESSMENT

Name	Station

	Low				High
I used my station time wisely.	1	2	3	4	5
I completed the station task.	1	2	3	4	5
I understood the objectives of the station.	1	2	3	4	5

What I learned:

Some questions I have:

J.3 QUALITY WORK CRITERIA

Following are some ideas to help students define "quality" and these criteria can be used in rubrics.

Quality Writing Project

- ➤ High level content
- ➤ Meaningful details
- ➤ Neat/Organized/Typed
- ➤ Writing conventions followed

Quality (Skit/Play)

- ➤ Memorize script
- ➤ Costumes/Props
- ➤ Well acted
- ➤ Can be heard clearly

Quality (Poster/Visual)

- ➤ Vivid colors
- ➤ Flow
- ➤ Easy to read
- ➤ Unique/clear message

Quality (Song)

- ➤ Original
- ➤ Taped/Live/Video
- ➤ Costumes/Instruments
- ➤ Loud and clear voice

Quality (Children's Book)

- ➤ Colorful, well drawn pictures
- ➤ Language/content appropriate for age group
- ➤ Cover page attractive
- ➤ Writing conventions followed

Group Work (high to low)

- ➤ Encourages others; collaborates and resolves conflicts
- ➤ Listens well; helps others; shares
- ➤ Appropriate effort, cooperative
- ➤ Inappropriate effort; not cooperative

Work Habits

- ➤ Uses time well, self-motivated, effort beyond average
- ➤ Time on task, appropriate effort
- ➤ Little time on task or effort
- ➤ Not working, resistant

Presentation

- ➤ Dynamic and compelling
- ➤ Interest holding
- ➤ Not so interesting
- ➤ Sleep inducing

Effort and Preparation

- ➤ Considerable
- ➤ More than average
- ➤ Sufficient
- ➤ Minimal or none

Visual Aids

- ➤ Extensive, attractive, enhances information
- ➤ Appropriate number and quality, works with information
- ➤ Few in number and quality, little value
- ➤ Minimal or none

J.4 C U KAN RUBRIC TEMPLATE

Expectations	Amazing	Above Average	Average	Awful
Understand _____ pts.	• Shows complex understanding of the concepts • Supports with data from text • Explores related ideas _____ pts.	• Understands the concepts • Uses some text references • Explores ideas beyond facts and details ____ pts.	• Limited understanding of key concepts • Limited text reference • Little depth or elaboration of idea ____ pts.	• Little understanding of the concept • No or inaccurate reference to text ____ pts.
Know _____ pts.	• Precise facts • In depth and well supported ____ pts.	• Covers facts effectively • Well developed ____ pts.	• Valid facts but little depth or elaboration ____ pts.	• Needs more facts • Needs accurate facts ____ pts.
Quality Work (as defined by your group; see below) _____ pts.	• Met quality work criteria • Unique, fresh, or imaginative work ____ pts.	• Met quality work criteria • Creatively integrated work ____ pts.	• Met quality work criteria ____ pts.	• Did not meet quality work criteria ____ pts.
_____ pts.	_____ pts.	____ pts.	____ pts.	____ pts.

Ways I/We Will Do Quality Work for Our Project: _____

1. _____
2. _____
3. _____

What we did that was Quality Work: What we can improve upon next time:

Student Grade: _____   **Teacher Grade:** _____

COMMENTS:

J.5 EARLY ELEMENTARY RUBRIC TEMPLATE

Name: _____

How I Did	Good	Not So Good
Understands	🙂	🙁
Knows	🙂	🙁
Good Presentation (Quality Work)	🙂	🙁

Teacher Comments:

K.1 FURTHER READINGS: GENERAL

Chapman, C., & Freeman, L. (1996). *Multiple intelligences centers and projects.* Arlington Heights, IL: Skylight Training and Publishing, Inc.

Cohen, E. G. (1994). *Designing groupwork: Strategies for the heterogeneous classroom* (2nd ed.). New York: Teachers College Press.

Erickson, H. L. (2000). *Stirring the head, heart and soul: Redefining curriculum and instruction.* (2nd ed.). Thousand Oaks, CA: Corwin Press.

Glasser, W. (1993). *The quality school teacher.* New York: Harper-Collins.

Gregory, G., & Chapman, C. (2002). *Differentiated instructional strategies: One size doesn't fit all.* Thousand Oaks, CA: Corwin Press.

Jensen, E. (1998). *Teaching with the brain in mind.* Alexandria, VA: Association for Supervision and Curriculum Development.

Jensen, E. (2000). *Different brains, different learners: How to reach the hard to reach.* San Diego: The Brain Store.

Kingore, B. (2002). *Rubrics and more!* Austin, TX: Professional Associates Publishing.

Kottler, E. (2002). *Children with limited English: Teaching strategies for the regular classroom.* Thousand Oaks, CA: Corwin Press.

Silver, H., Strong, R., & Perini, M. (2000). *So each may learn: Integrating learning styles and multiple intelligences.* Alexandria, VA: Association for Supervision and Curriculum Development.

Tomlinson, C. A. (2001). *How to differentiate instruction in mixed-ability classrooms* (2nd ed.). Alexandria, VA: Association for Supervision and Curriculum Development.

Tomlinson, C. A. (2004). *Fulfilling the promise of the differentiated classroom: Strategies and tools for responsive teaching.* Alexandria, VA: Association for Supervision and Curriculum Development.

Weinbrenner, S. (1996). *Teaching kids with learning difficulties in the regular classroom.* Minneapolis, MN: Free Spirit Publishing.

Weinbrenner, S. (2001). *Teaching gifted kids in the regular classroom.* Minneapolis, MN: Free Spirit Publishing.

Wolfe, P. (2001). *Brain matters: Translating research into classroom practice.* Alexandria, VA: Association for Supervision and Curriculum Development.

K.2 VARIED LEVEL TEXTS

Lerner Classroom
www.lernerclassroom.com
Leveled Nonfiction Books & Teaching Guides
Social Studies, Science, Reading/Literacy
K–8

Redbrick
www.redbricklearning.com
Leveled Nonfiction
K–8

National Geographic
www.nationalgeographic.com/education
Nonfiction Literacy Catalog
Reading Comprehension, Expository Writing, Differentiated Theme Sets
K–12

Time for Kids
www.teachercreated.com
Exploring Nonfiction: Reading in the Content Areas
K–12

Pearson AFS Globe
www.agsglobe.com
Middle and High School High-Low Text Resources
6–12

References

Association for Supervision and Curriculum Development. (2007). *Report on the commission for the whole child*. Alexandria, VA: Author.

Association of Graduate Careers Advisory Services. (2005). First impressions. *The interview itself*. Retrieved May 6, 2006, from http://www.prospects.ac.uk/cms/ShowPage/Home_page/Applications_and_interviews/Interviews/The_inter view_itself/p!elpgeg

Biancarosa, C., & Snow, C. E. (2006). *Reading next – A vision for action and research in middle and high school literacy: A report to Carnegie Corporation of New York* (2nd ed.). Washington, DC: Alliance for Excellent Education.

Collins, A., Brown, J. S., & Newman, S. E. (1989). Cognitive apprenticeship: Teaching the craft of reading, writing, and mathematics. In L. B. Resnick (Ed.), *Knowing, learning, and instruction: Essays in honor of Robert Glaser* (pp. 453–494). Hillsdale, NJ: Lawrence Erlbaum Associates.

Collins, A., Brown, J. S., & Newman, S. E. (in press). Cognitive apprenticeship: Teaching the craft of reading, writing, and mathematics (2nd ed.). In L. B. Resnick (Ed.), *Knowing, learning, and instruction: Essays in honor of Robert Glaser*. Hillsdale, NJ: Lawrence Erlbaum Associates.

Jensen, E. (1998). *Teaching with the brain in mind*. Alexandria, VA: Association for Supervision and Curriculum Development.

Klem, A. M., & Connell, J. P. (2004). Relationships matter: Linking teacher support to student engagement and achievement. *Journal of School Health, 74* (7), 262–273.

Pearson, P. D., & Gallagher, M. (1983). The instruction of reading comprehension. *Contemporary Educational Psychology*, Vol 8.

Pink, D. (2005). *A Whole New Mind: Moving from the information age to the conceptual age*. New York: Penguin Group.

Reading next: A vision for action and research in middle and high school literacy. (2004). The Carnegie Corporation of New York and the Alliance for Excellence in Education. Retrieved May 6, 2006, from http://www.a114ed.org/publications/ReadingNext/index.html

Secretan, L. (2004). *Inspire: What great leaders do*. Hoboken, NJ: John Wiley & Sons.

Sousa, D. (2000). *How the brain learns*. Thousand Oaks, CA: Corwin Press.

Tomlinson, C. A. (1999). *The differentiated classroom: Responding to the needs of all learners*. Alexandria, VA: Association for Supervision and Curriculum Development.

Tomlinson, C. A., & McTighe, J. (2006). *Integrating differentiated instruction + understanding by design*. Alexandria, VA. Association for Supervision and Curriculum Development.

Vygotsky, L. (1978). *Mind in society: The development of higher psychological processes*. Cambridge, MA: Harvard University Press.

Wiggins, G., & McTighe, J. (1998). *Understanding by design*. Alexandria, VA: Association for Supervision and Curriculum Development.

Index

CORWIN PRESS

The Corwin Press logo—a raven striding across an open book—represents the union of courage and learning. Corwin Press is committed to improving education for all learners by publishing books and other professional development resources for those serving the field of PreK–12 education. By providing practical, hands-on materials, Corwin Press continues to carry out the promise of its motto: **"Helping Educators Do Their Work Better."**